# How to use Ex

## In this issue

The 90 daily readings in this issue of *Explore* are designed to help you understand and apply the Bible as you read it each day.

## It's serious!

We suggest that you allow 15 minutes each day to work through the Bible passage with the notes. It should be a meal, not a snack! Readings from other parts of the Bible can throw valuable light on the study passage. These cross-references can be skipped if you are already feeling full up, but they will expand your grasp of the Bible. *Explore* uses the NIV Bible translation, but you can also use it with the ESV or another translation of your choice.

Sometimes a prayer section will encourage you to stop and pray through the application of God's word—but it is always important to allow time to pray for God's Spirit to bring his word to life, and to shape the way we think and live.

## We're serious!

All of us who work on *Explore* share a passion for getting the Bible into people's lives. We passionately hold to the Bible as God's word—to honour and follow, not to explain away.

**1** Find a time you can read the Bible each day

**2** Find a place where you can be quiet and think

**3** Ask God to help you understand

**4** Carefully read through the Bible passage for today

**5** Study the verses with Explore, taking time to think

**6** Pray about what you have read

the**good**book
COMPANY

*Opening up the Bible*

# Welcome to Explore

Being a Christian isn't a skill you learn, like carpentry or flower arranging. Nor is it a lifestyle choice, like the kind of clothes you wear, or the people you choose to hang out with. It's about having a real relationship with the living God through his Son, Jesus Christ. The Bible tells us that this relationship is like a marriage.

It's important to start with this, because many Christians view the practice of daily Bible-reading as a Christian duty, or a hard discipline that is just one more thing to get done in our busy modern lives.

But the Bible is God speaking to us: opening his mind to us on how he thinks, what he wants for us and what his plans are for the world. And most importantly, it tells us what he has done for us in sending his Son, Jesus Christ, into the world. It's the way the Spirit shows Jesus to us, and changes us as we behold his glory.

The Bible is not a manual. It's a love letter. And as with any love letter, we'll want to treasure it, and make time to read and re-read it, so we know we are loved, and discover how we can please the one who loves us. Here are a few suggestions for making your daily time with God more of a joy than a burden:

🞂 *Time:* Find a time when you will not be disturbed, and when the cobwebs are cleared from your mind. Many people have found that the morning is the best time as it sets you up for the day. If you're not a "morning person", then last thing at night or a mid-morning break might suit you. Whatever works for you is right for you.

🞂 *Place:* Jesus says that we are not to make a great show of our religion *(see Matthew 6:5-6)*, but rather, to pray with the door to our room shut. Some people plan to get to work a few minutes earlier and get their Bible out in an office or some other quiet corner.

🞂 *Prayer:* Although *Explore* helps with specific prayer ideas from the passage, try to develop your own lists to pray through. Use the flap inside the back cover to help with this. And allow what you read in the Scriptures to shape what you pray for yourself, the world and others.

🞂 *Share:* As the saying goes—*expression deepens impression.* So try to cultivate the habit of sharing with others what you have learned. Why not join our Facebook group to share your encouragements, questions and prayer requests? Search for *Explore: For your daily walk with God.*

And remember, *it's quality, not quantity, that counts:* better to think briefly about a single verse than to skim through pages without absorbing anything. It's about developing your relationship with the living God. The sign that your daily time with God is real is when you start to love him more and serve him more wholeheartedly.

*Tim Thornborough and Carl Laferton*
*Editors*

# Death without decay

*Death can seem a hopeless prospect and can make life appear meaningless. We need to take to heart David's reflections on a God-directed life and a God-filled death.*

**Read Psalm 16**

## The source of hope

❷ *How does David express:*
- *his weakness and need (v 1)?*
- *his own standing before God (v 2, v 5)?*
- *his delight in God's presence (v 7-8)?*

❷ *Where does he find direction, joy and pleasure (v 11)?*

❷ *How does this kind of attitude towards God shape David's attitude towards God's people (v 3)?*

❷ *What is his attitude to those who are rejecting God (v 4)?*

## ▾ Apply

❷ *Can you say, and mean, verse 2?*

❷ *Of what else, or who else, are you tempted to say: "You are what directs my life; you are what I most need in life"?*

Often we equate success with lasting satisfaction. But verse 11 reminds us that "joy" and "pleasures" are really only found in living with God as Lord.

❷ *Do you need to turn away from chasing personal glory?*

## Eternal hope

**Re-read Psalm 16:9-11**

❷ *What does David know about his future?*

Ultimate hope comes in verse 10: "You will not abandon me to the realm of the dead, nor will you let your faithful one see decay".

**Read Acts 2:24-32**

❷ *What event was David looking towards in Psalm 16:10?*

❷ *So where is David ultimately looking for eternal life and lasting joy?*

What faithful David looked forward to, we look back on as believers today. Our confidence in life and in death does not come from ourselves, but from the one who conquered the grave and is Lord of life.

## ▴ Pray

As we embark on another new year, scan through your plans and think about what you hope to achieve in it, and the people you want to serve, love and help.

Commit the coming year to the Lord in the knowledge that he is your salvation and hope.

# Badly treated

*When you're badly treated—when people sin against you—what is your natural reaction towards those who are abusing you?*

## Listening
### Read Psalm 17:1-6

- ❓ *What does David ask (v 1, 6)?*
- ❓ *What does he know about his own conduct (v 3-5)? Why does this matter?*
- ❓ *What is most important to David (v 2)?*

God's people live repentant lives. We should never want any sin to be lingering unnoticed. Before we point the finger at others, we need to examine ourselves.

## ⌃ Pray

If, as you look at your life over the last week, you can't say what David can say here of his own conduct, then spend some time confessing how:

- your mouth has sinned (v 3).
- you haven't followed God's way (v 5).

## Sheltering
### Read Psalm 17:7-12

- ❓ *What is David asking for (v 7-9)?*

God is glorified—the wonder of his love is shown—when we come to him in weakness and he acts for us in strength.

## Receiving help
### Read Psalm 17:13-15

God's sovereign will is what brings about changes in our circumstances.

- ❓ *Who does David recognise will be the victor in his struggle?*

There are two ways to live in this world: like David, seeking to live for God and trusting him to provide, or like David's opponents. While David's future is wonderful (remember Psalm 16), those who live without God know only the partial, fleeting joys of this life (Psalm 17:14).

David is totally satisfied with "seeing" God (v 15)—with knowing and being known by him.

Facing what is a challenging time, sinned against by those around him, he knows that one day he will be perfectly righteous, and will be in God's presence. And this hope is for us who are in Christ today.

## ⌄ Apply

Are you reflecting on the hope of heaven as you struggle with difficult people and challenging situations in the present?

Fast forward to heaven in your heart as you face the difficulties of the present. And remember what Psalm 17 teaches us when we are being sinned against: to examine ourselves, to pray, and to trust in God's sovereign hand at work in us, and in the world.

# 1 CORINTHIANS:
# The trouble with idolatry

We now enter the fourth block of material in 1 Corinthians: chapters 11 – 14, on corporate worship.

**Read 1 Corinthians 11:2-16**

Scholars continue to debate various questions that arise from this fiendishly difficult passage. So get ready...

## Honour and shame

To most of us, the "head" is the one in charge. But the heart of Paul's picture isn't command and control. It's honour and shame—like in an eastern family. The "head" is not primarily the one in charge, but the prominent one: the one whose reputation is either honoured or shamed by the actions of others.

❓ *In verses 3-6, what does Paul say would bring disgrace or dishonour? Who to?*

## Men and women

This might all sound arbitrary: why should a head covering bring disgrace? Paul is arguing that there are differences between men and women, which are reflected in their appearances. Different cultures have different customs about the appearance of men and women, but it all stems from the fact that God created us as different (v 7-9).

Paul doesn't say that only men bear the image of God, or that women are inferior. Both bear God's image, and reflect God's glory on earth in complementary ways. Don't forget that Paul is talking about what women should wear while praying and prophesying in the church—he's not writing women off!

❓ *How does Paul underline the interdependence of the sexes in verses 11-12?*

## The nature of things

Paul's final argument is based on what the Corinthians already accepted as natural. Society's assumption was that long hair was proper for a woman but a disgrace for a man (v 13-14). Therefore it's obvious to say that men shouldn't have their heads covered (as if by long hair), and women should.

## ☑ Apply

How do we apply Paul's teaching today? We need to "translate" the symbols here from the ancient Corinthian culture into our own.

Paul's intention is to preserve appropriate distinctions between the sexes, and to avoid a sexually provocative or maritally inappropriate appearance in gathered worship. This brings glory to God, honour to both men and women, and unity to the church.

❓ *How might we communicate those things in our culture?*
❓ *In general in your relationships with the opposite sex, how can you reflect the fact that men and women are different but not independent?*

# Communion chaos

*What was the most disorganised or chaotic Christian meeting you've ever been in? What happened?*

There are a lot of ways in which our Christian meetings can be fairly disastrous. But most of us have never thought what Paul says about communion at Corinth: "Your meetings do more harm than good" (11:17)!

It reflects how serious the Lord's Supper is. This is the body and blood of Jesus. We are treading on holy ground.

## Together, apart
**Read 1 Corinthians 11:17-27**

❷ *What's the fundamental problem in Corinth (v 18)?*
❷ *What's their motivation (v 19)?*

We've already seen other divisions in the Corinthian church. But in this case, division completely changes the nature of what they are doing.

❷ *What's happening (v 20-22)?*
❷ *Why is it "not the Lord's Supper" they are eating?*

## The real meaning

Paul's marvellous summary paragraph in verses 23-26 shows us what we actually do as we celebrate the Lord's Supper.

❷ *What do we look back to?*
❷ *What do we celebrate about the present?*
❷ *What do we look forward to in the future?*

**TIME OUT**

Look back to 10:16-17.

❷ *What other meanings in the Lord's Supper does Paul draw out here?*

## Be warned

❷ *How does Paul show his disgust at what the Corinthian Christians are doing (11:17, 22, 27)?*
❷ *Based on Paul's description of the Lord's Supper, why do you think he was so unimpressed?*

## ✔ Apply

❷ *In your church, is the Lord's Supper a genuine sign of unity?*
❷ *How else can we express unity and make sure everyone is included when we gather as a church?*
❷ *What can you specifically do to help with this?*
❷ *What else in what Paul says in verses 23-26 do you think needs to be expressed as churches gather and eat together?*

# Two types of judgment

*Communion is meaningful and powerful, and the Corinthians are bungling it.*

It's not surprising that what comes next is a call for repentance and a warning of judgment.

### Read 1 Corinthians 11:28-34

Paul has already said that if we take communion "in an unworthy manner"—that is, without having repented of our sin—we will be "guilty of sinning against the body and blood of the Lord" (v 27). That sounds serious, and indeed it is.

❓ *So what does Paul call us to do (v 28)?*

This is not a call for moral perfection. It's not aimed at excluding those who have sinned. It's aimed at excluding those who do not care whether or not they have sinned.

This is what it means to discern "the body of Christ" (v 29)—to recognise that we need Jesus' death to cover our sin. As Question 81 of the Heidelberg Catechism puts it, those who should come to the Lord's Table are "those who are displeased with themselves because of their sins, but who nevertheless trust that their sins are pardoned and that their remaining weakness is covered by the suffering and death of Christ".

❓ *If you take the Lord's Supper without repenting, what are you doing (v 29)?*
❓ *Paul clarifies what he means by that in verse 30. What judgment does he mean?*

Modern readers often find this astonishing, even shocking. Is Paul really saying that God might make a person physically unwell, or even kill them, as an act of judgment for dishonouring him? Indeed he is.

But notice why.

❓ *What is God saving those he disciplines from (v 32)?*

## ⌃ Pray

Do you think God is using the circumstances in your life to discipline you at the moment? What could he be saying to you? Spend some time in prayer, asking God to help you see your sin and turn from it.

Confess your sins and spend some time praising God for his mercy.

## ⌄ Apply

Paul summarises his instructions in verses 33-34: eat together, rather than some wolfing everything down and leaving others without.

Think about how you celebrate communion in your church.

❓ *What is said beforehand?*
❓ *What do you think about as you take the bread and wine?*
❓ *How could you make sure you do this in a worthy manner—both personally and corporately?*
❓ *How else can you express your unity as a church, and the mercy and grace of God as you meet together?*

*Bible in a year: Genesis 13-15 • Romans 5* ✔

# Now about the gifts...

*It's time for Paul to deal with a fresh question from the Corinthians: what about spiritual gifts?*

❓ *What do you think of when you hear the phrase "spiritual gifts"?*

❓ *Look ahead at 1 Corinthians 12:28. Do you have experience of these things? What do you understand them to mean?*

❓ *How do you think we can tell whether a particular gift really comes from the Lord?*

## The first test

### Read 1 Corinthians 12:1-6

❓ *What's Paul's aim here (v 1)?*

❓ *What do the Corinthians already know (v 2)?*

❓ *But what else does he want them to know (v 3)?*

The acid test of whether the Holy Spirit is at work is the declaration of the lordship of Jesus. That might not be the first test we would think of. It certainly doesn't seem to be what the Corinthians thought. They were impressed by miraculous power, prophetic insight, faith that can move mountains and the languages of men and angels—and so are many of us today.

For Paul, however, the Spirit's activity is shown in a much more foundational way. If a person curses Jesus, they are not speaking by the Spirit (even if they appear to have great power). If a person declares, "Jesus is Lord," they are speaking by the Spirit (even if they don't appear to have great power).

## Three in one

❓ *How do we see the unity of the Trinity in verse 3?*

❓ *What about in verses 4-6?*

❓ *What does that suggest about how we should exercise spiritual gifts?*

The Trinity collaborate together, and therefore the activity of the Spirit should not be divorced from the work of the Father and the Son. This introduces the idea that will dominate the rest of chapter 12: unity in diversity. In the world, diversity feels as if it is pulling against unity: either you remain united and squash your differences or you express your differences and break apart. In the church, it is different. Diversity serves unity, and unity celebrates diversity.

## ⌄ Apply

❓ *Based on what Paul says in these verses, where do you think you have seen the Spirit at work recently:*
- *in your own life?*
- *in the lives of others around you?*

❓ *How do you hope the Spirit might work in the future:*
- *in your own life?*
- *in the lives of others around you?*

# The common good

*Father, Son and Spirit work together. So should we…*

**Read 1 Corinthians 12:7-11**

The exaltation of Jesus as Lord is the clearest sign of the Spirit's work. But another clear indication is what Paul calls "the common good" (v 7). Spiritual gifts are given for the advantage of everybody in the church. The manifestation of the Spirit is given "to each one"— including you—for the benefit of everybody. (Although the word "manifestation" is sometimes associated with weird phenomena in the contemporary church, the word here, *phanerosis,* simply refers to the Spirit's power being disclosed, exhibited and put on display.)

## Nine gifts

To show what this looks like in a congregation, Paul gives a number of examples. It's important to stress that this is not a comprehensive list of every gift the Spirit might give.

*Messages of wisdom or knowledge.* This could refer to a whole range of things. Paul might mean preaching the gospel, or the God-given ability to read a situation and speak wisely and knowledgeably into it.

*Faith.* All faith is the result of the Spirit's work, but Paul is not talking about saving faith here; that is given to all believers, not just some. More likely, he means the gift of being able to believe God for apparently impossible things.

*Gifts of healing.* Although all believers can and should pray for healing, and elders in particular are called to do so (James 5:14-16), any healing is a gift from God—not, we should note, a reward for sufficient levels of godliness, certainty or technique—which some have far more than others.

*Miraculous powers.* Paul himself clearly worked miracles (Acts 19:11-12).

*Prophecy.* This probably means supernatural insight into a specific person's circumstances. (We'll talk more about this in later studies.)

*Distinguishing between spirits.* This is the ability to tell whether something is genuinely the work of the Spirit, or whether it is demonic, or coming from the spirit of the world, or something else.

*Speaking and interpreting tongues.* This seems to refer to a special prayer-language which is used primarily to speak to God (again, we'll see more of this later).

❷ *Who do each of these gifts come from (v 11)?*
❷ *Why does one person get one gift and another person get another (v 11)?*
❷ *What might it look like for each of these gifts to be used "for the common good"?*

## ◣ Pray

Ask God to work in you for the common good today and this week.

# One body, many parts

*Spiritual gifts are given to build unity, but so often they become a source of division. The next section of 1 Corinthians is a goldmine of wisdom for such problems.*

**Read 1 Corinthians 12:12-26**

Bodies are a magnificent metaphor for the church because they express unity-in-diversity like nothing else on earth. The body is one, not in spite of the fact that it has many different parts which all have different functions but because of it. Oneness is only possible because of "many-ness". The same is true of the church.

> ❓ *Why are we all one body (v 13)?*
> ❓ *But in what ways do we remain many?*

## Not less

> ❓ *Who do you know who might feel inferior or dismiss the gifts they've been given?*
> ❓ *But what two reasons does Paul give to show this is wrong (v 15-16, 17-19)?*
> ❓ *What would it be like if nobody had the gift the person feeling inferior has?*
> ❓ *What would it be like if everyone in your church had the same gift?*

## Not greater

> ❓ *Who do you know who might feel superior because of the gifts they've been given?*
> ❓ *What does this kind of person end up saying (v 21)?*
> ❓ *But why is this wrong too (v 22-24)?*

A true understanding of the body will produce humility. If we prioritise what is visible and impressive (preaching, prophesying), and demean what is invisible (helping, praying), we should remember that the truly indispensable parts of our bodies are the ones we don't think about (v 22). You can survive without an eye or a hand, but not without a liver.

## Unpresentable?

If anything, the fact that a body part is hidden away as unpresentable—Paul is talking about sexual organs now—is a sign of how special it is (v 23). In the same way, in the church, God has given "greater honour to the parts that lacked it" (v 24). So there should be no superiority, no smugness and no self-pity; every member is needed.

## ✓ Apply

> ❓ *Which trap are you most likely to fall into—thinking you're inferior or thinking you're superior? How does this passage help or challenge you?*
> ❓ *How does Paul apply his teaching in verses 25-26?*
> ❓ *How can you put this into practice in your church?*

# Strange love

*Psalm 17 was a plea for help in troubled times. Today's psalm is a song of triumph after troubled times. But the victor isn't really David.*

## God is my love
### Read Psalm 18:1-6

❷ *How does David express his love for and dependence on God (v 1-3)?*
❷ *What does David seem to have escaped from?*
❷ *How might these truths about God reassure those who are in need?*

This is the first time in the Psalms (indeed in the whole Bible) where the writer describes his relationship and response to God as one of love. Few devotees of other religions would dare to make such a shocking statement as this. But the word "love" carries a variety of meanings in our language. So what exactly does it mean?

Surely David did not have in mind the gooey sentimentality that many associate with the word. Nor is it the flag-waving supporter kind of emotion—*I love watching Manchester United play*—which delivers enjoyment, but can be done from an uninvolved distance. This love is one that encompasses mind, body, soul and strength. It sees all that God is and has done for him, and longs to serve and please him in response.

#### TIME OUT

Paul compares the relationship of man and wife to the relationship between Jesus and his people (see Ephesians 5:21-33). He should love her like Christ does; she should love him like the church loves its Lord. This

actually applies to both men and women in different ways, but when a wife says: "I love you"—what does she mean? And how are these related to the way we love Christ?

- *Admiration*: she not only is attracted to his physical qualities, but more importantly his character.
- *Gratitude*: her love and confidence grow as she is nurtured by her lover, and rejoices that she is blessed to be with him.
- *Humility*: her love is demonstrated by respect, deference and service to him—she loves him by living to please him.
- *A willingness to commit*: she bonds to him for life.

## ⌄ Apply

David was facing a specific historical situation (see the intro to the psalm). Jonah used Psalm 18:4-6 to praise God for sending a fish to rescue him (Jonah 2:1-10). We're not opposed by a murderous madman (Saul), nor in the belly of a fish, yet these words are ours as much as David's and Jonah's:

❷ *How is Psalm 18:4-6 true of every Christian?*

## ⌃ Pray

Can you say verse 1 honestly to God? And mean more than a shallow "feel-good" emotion? Now would be a great time to express this to him.

*Bible in a year: Genesis 23-24 • Romans 8:22-39*

# All must have prizes?

*That's what the Dodo in "Alice in Wonderland" says at the end of a race which nobody has won. We might expect a similar conclusion to Paul's words in 1 Corinthians 12.*

Every gift is as important as every other. No part of the body is more vital than any other. That's what Paul has been saying, isn't it?

Actually, he has a surprise for us.

**Read 1 Corinthians 12:27-31**

On the one hand, he remains absolutely clear on the interdependence of the body, our need for each other, and the fact that nobody can thrive without drawing on the gifts of everyone else. No gift is common to everybody.

> ❷ *How do we see the equality of believers in these verses?*
> ❷ *How does Paul show that we need one another?*

## The greater gifts

Yet Paul also believes that some gifts take precedence over others. He urges them to "eagerly desire the greater gifts" (v 31), and puts several of the gifts in order (v 28).

This simply reflects the reality of what bodies are like: all parts are equally valuable and equally part of the body, but there are some that you simply cannot live without (a heart, a brain) and some that you can (an ear, a leg).

> ❷ *Look at the order in which Paul places the gifts in verse 28. Are there any surprises? What order of importance would you have chosen?*

Paul puts apostles first, then prophets (getting us ready for the command to pursue prophecy "eagerly" and "especially" in 14:1), then teachers. After that he lists four gifts without numbering them—mixing ones that might seem very impressive and dramatic with ones that might seem more ordinary and everyday. Finally, he puts the gift with which the Corinthians were most obsessed, namely tongue-speaking, last.

## ✔ Apply

> ❷ *What will it look like for you to "eagerly desire" the gifts which Paul puts first in his list? How could you take steps to pursue and grow in those gifts?*
> ❷ *What gifts in this list do you think God has given you already? How can you use these gifts for the good of others in the body of Christ?*

## And yet

The stage is set for Paul to bring some more specific application to the way the spiritual gifts are to be used in corporate worship.

Before doing that, however, he wants to ensure that the motive for using the gifts—and in fact the motive for everything we do in the Christian life—is properly established. Spiritual gifts are wonderful, but Paul wants us to know that there is something more excellent (12:31)...

# The most excellent way

*The words of 1 Corinthians 13 have been read billions of times: privately and publicly, on radio and television, in churches and on film.*

They risk becoming domesticated, or even meaningless, through over-familiarity. Yet I wonder how many people who hear them, or even read them aloud at weddings, know why they talk about "the tongues of men or of angels" and "the gift of prophecy" and "all mysteries and all knowledge" and "faith that can move mountains" (v 1-2) or have any idea that they were originally written about spiritual gifts. Not many, I suspect.

**Read 1 Corinthians 13:1-13**

- ❷ *What do the Corinthians seem to be most impressed by (v 1-3)?*
- ❷ *But what does Paul say about those things?*

No matter what our church background is, our go-to hallmarks of spirituality are put firmly in their place here.

## All you need is love

- ❷ *What do you think people today mean by "love"?*
- ❷ *What does Paul say love is like (v 4, 6-7)?*
- ❷ *What does he say love is not like (v 4-6)?*

## ⌃ Pray

Take some time to reflect on Paul's description in verses 4-7.

As you pray, consider your relationships with friends, family, colleagues and fellow church members. Ask God to show you where you are failing to love as you should, and to help you express the kind of love Paul describes.

## When fullness comes

In context, these searching and beautiful words are primarily designed to help churches use spiritual gifts wisely.

- ❷ *What is the difference between love and the spiritual gifts (v 8-10)?*
- ❷ *In what sense are the spiritual gifts like the words and thoughts of a child (v 11)?*
- ❷ *In what sense are the spiritual gifts like seeing a reflection in a mirror (v 12)?*
- ❷ *What are we looking forward to that is better than the spiritual gifts (v 12)?*
- ❷ *What will remain (v 13)?*

Language like this can only refer to the return of Christ and the renewal of all things, when we will see Jesus face to face. On that day, the partial and temporary will no longer be needed, like stars fading into the background in the light of the rising sun.

## ⌄ Apply

- ❷ *How can you prioritise love over all things this week?*

# An eager desire

*What's the most encouraging thing anyone has ever said to you?*

**Read 1 Corinthians 14:1-5**

- ❓ *What are we to eagerly desire (v 1)?*
- ❓ *What's our ruling principle as we do so (v 1)?*

Some Christians argue that Paul's instructions here do not apply to us today. Essentially that's because they believe "prophecy" must mean infallible divine revelation—which ceased after the completion of the New Testament and the death of the apostles. But it seems clear to me that that is not what Paul means by prophecy here.

## The greater gift

Paul's purpose in chapter 14 is to commend the gift of prophecy, and particularly to commend it as more useful in public contexts than the gift of languages. By all accounts the Corinthians were obsessed with languages, and Paul wants to reorder their preferences.

- ❓ *If you speak in a tongue, who are you speaking to and how (v 2)?*
- ❓ *What's the result (v 4)?*
- ❓ *What's different about prophecy (v 4)? Why?*
- ❓ *Why should that make prophecy more desirable as a gift (v 4-5)?*

## What is prophecy?

This gives us a very helpful start when it comes to understanding what prophecy is, at least in the context of this letter. Prophetic speech is directed towards people, and it strengthens, encourages and comforts us. The rest of the chapter will fill out the picture.

## ☑ Apply

- ❓ *According to what Paul says here, do you think you have ever prophesied?*
- ❓ *Have you ever heard other people prophesying, according to Paul's definition?*
- ❓ *Have you heard people claim that something is prophecy that doesn't fit into Paul's definition?*
- ❓ *What will it look like for you to "eagerly desire" prophecy?*
- ❓ *Who could you encourage, strengthen or comfort today?*

## ⌃ Pray

Ask God for the gift of prophecy. Try praying for a particular person or group of people. How might God lead you to build them up with your words?

# Babbling voices

*"If I speak in the tongues of men or of angels, but do not have love, I am only a resounding gong or a clanging cymbal," wrote Paul in 1 Corinthians 13:1.*

Now he's going to explain more of what he means.

He spends the next 14 verses talking about how to speak (and how not to speak) in languages, before moving back to prophecy in the second half of the chapter.

Paul's problem is with the self-indulgent use of languages in public meetings, without interpretation, without any regard for unbelievers and without consideration for the rest of the church. We are beginning to see why he spent so long talking about love (13:1-13) before addressing the use of this specific gift.

### Read 1 Corinthians 14:6-19

- ❓ *What's wrong with a harp that doesn't play distinct notes (v 6-7)?*
- ❓ *What's the effect of a trumpet that makes no clear sound (v 8)?*
- ❓ *How do these images explain to us the problem with speaking in tongues (v 6, 9)?*

The purpose of a gift in the gathered church is to edify people, not to parade our spirituality, and gifts can't be edifying if they aren't intelligible. A person burbling away in tongues in a public meeting, without interpretation, doesn't edify anyone.

## Meaningless

The Greek word *glossa* can be translated either "tongue" or "language". It's the normal word you would use for English, Mandarin, Swahili and so on. For Paul, the reality that the Corinthians are speaking a language (as opposed to a sequence of nonsensical noises) is very important. His argument in verses 10-11 runs like this: the world is full of languages, and they all mean something, and the whole point of speaking them is to be understood. It's the same in the church (v 12).

- ❓ *So what should tongue-speakers do (v 13)?*
- ❓ *How will this benefit them (v 15)?*
- ❓ *How will it benefit others (v 16-17)?*

Despite the practice in some churches of calling out in tongues and leaving the interpretation to someone else, Paul says it is our responsibility, when we speak in languages, to interpret what we have said (unless we know there is someone else around who can interpret).

- ❓ *How does Paul feel about speaking in tongues privately (v 18-19)?*
- ❓ *Why, do you think?*

## ✔ Apply

- ❓ *Does this passage challenge your views on speaking in tongues? Who could you discuss this with?*
- ❓ *Do your words generally build others up and edify them? How can you seek to do so more in everything you say?*

# Judgment or worship?

*If you didn't know Christ, what would you think if you saw someone speaking in tongues or prophesying in church?*

**Read 1 Corinthians 14:20-25**

❓ *What's Paul's goal in this paragraph (v 20)?*

He's contrasting maturity with immaturity. By running after the gift of languages without regard for anyone else, the Corinthians are being childish. They need to grow up.

## A sign for unbelievers

Paul next quotes Isaiah 28:11-12.

❓ *What did the Lord (through Isaiah) say would happen (1 Corinthians 14:21)?*

God would judge the unbelieving Israelites by speaking to them through foreigners who would rule over them.

So when Paul says that tongues are "a sign ... for unbelievers" (v 22), he is talking about a sign of judgment. The experience of being spoken to in languages you don't understand serves to emphasise your distance from God, just as it did for Israel.

❓ *Why is prophecy different (v 22)?*

By speaking in uninterpreted tongues in the church, the Corinthians are (unintentionally) pronouncing judgment over one another.

## Hope for enquirers

Paul's next words appear at first sight to be saying the exact opposite of what he's just said. But if we take "a sign for unbelievers"

to mean judgment, it makes sense. Now he is no longer talking about unbelievers who are destined for judgment. He's talking about "enquirers or unbelievers"—those who haven't yet believed but may come to do so.

❓ *What will happen when such enquirers hear tongues (v 23)?*
❓ *What will happen when they hear prophecy (v 24-25)?*

One of my favourite examples of this comes from someone who knew the Victorian preacher Charles Spurgeon:

*"Mr Spurgeon looked at me as if he knew me, and in his sermon he pointed to me [and] said that I took ninepence the Sunday before, and that there was fourpence profit out of it ... How he should know that, I could not tell. Then it struck me that it was God who had spoken to my soul through him." (The Autobiography of Charles H. Spurgeon, 2:226-27)*

Spiritual gifts are not just given to strengthen the church but to reveal the presence and holiness of God to unbelievers.

## ⌃ Pray

Pray for those you know who don't yet believe in Christ.

Pray for those who do know Christ, that they would be selfless as they exercise spiritual gifts, and that God would use their words to bring others to worship him.

# Building together

*Until now, Paul has been establishing principles. But in today's passage he gets to the practical application.*

......................................................................................................................................................................

**Read 1 Corinthians 14:26**

> ❓ *What does Paul say happens when Christians come together?*

This reveals a huge amount about early Christian worship. Everyone has been given spiritual gifts for the common good—they don't reside just with a pastor, or a group of elders. So Corinthian worship involved contributions from all sorts of people.

To some of us that sounds like paradise; to others it sounds like mayhem!

> ❓ *What's Paul's anchoring principle for what goes on in churches?*
> ❓ *How do you think that principle might prevent mayhem?*

## When to stay silent

**Read 1 Corinthians 14:27-33**

> ❓ *How do the commands in the following verses apply Paul's key principle?*
> • *v 27-28*
> • *v 29*
> • *v 30-31*

In a church with at least 50 members, and possibly quite a few more, this means that the vast majority will say nothing: not because we do not have gifts to use, but because our goal is edification, not self-expression.

Paul doesn't elaborate on how to "weigh" a prophecy. We can assume it would involve considering how it lines up with Scripture, whether it exalts Jesus as Lord, and whether it edifies the body.

This process is important, and it is also possible. Prophesying is not an ecstatic, out-of-body experience in which the speaker has no control over their body or their speech (v 32). Anyone who claims otherwise is not speaking by the Spirit. Spiritual gifts should never lead to chaos. "For God is not a God of disorder but of peace" (v 33).

## ✓ Apply

Think about an ordinary worship service at your church.

> ❓ *What are the similarities with what Paul describes?*
> ❓ *What are the differences?*
> ❓ *What are some other ways in which Jesus is exalted as Lord, unity is expressed, and the body of Christ is built up?*

Then think about your own contributions at such services.

> ❓ *What contributions, if any, do you make to church meetings?*
> ❓ *What has been your motivation so far?*
> ❓ *Do you think you should speak less, or more?*
> ❓ *Do you think you should speak in a different way?*

# What the...?

*There are some parts of the Bible, and of Paul's letters, about which people say, "Surely it can't mean **that**".*

Usually, that's because we don't like it. We read something that doesn't fit with our modern sensibilities, so we do a huge amount of work to try and make it look as if it means something else. But sometimes it's based on the text itself. Something the passage, or the book as a whole, makes it clear that the obvious interpretation is not actually correct.

Nowhere is this truer than of Paul's statement in 1 Corinthians 14:34.

## Asking questions

**Read 1 Corinthians 14:34-40**

Paul recently spent 15 verses on the question of what women should wear over their heads while praying or prophesying in the church service (11:2-16), which would make no sense whatsoever if women were prohibited from public speech. He has also spent much of the last few chapters explaining how "each one" in the congregation has a gift, and how "each one" can and should use it. So he cannot mean that women are not allowed to speak at all.

One possibility is that Paul is prohibiting women specifically from the weighing of prophecy (14:29-30) because it involves a governmental responsibility that Paul limits to the fathers (or elders) of the church. Another possibility is that some women at Corinth were in the habit of interrupting their husbands while they were prophesy-

ing. Paul will not allow this because it is not submissive or honourable, and it leads to disorder rather than peace.

I take the second view—which fits well with the next sentence, where women are told to ask questions "at home" (v 35).

## A strong appeal

❓ *What are the answers to Paul's rhetorical questions in verse 36?*

No matter how prophetic or spiritually gifted the Corinthians may think they are, they cannot simply do their own thing here; it is a command of the Lord himself (v 37), and anyone who ignores it will be ignored themselves (v 38). Prophecy is a wonderful gift, but it should never lead to anyone setting aside the law (v 34), the gospel (v 36), or Jesus' commands through his apostles (v 37).

## ⌄ Apply

Re-read Paul's concluding words in verses 39-40.

❓ *What challenge do these words pose to your church?*

## ⌃ Pray

Pray for the worldwide church. Ask God to bring unity, wisdom, peace and edification to his people.

# The gospel in miniature

*If someone asked you to explain briefly what "the gospel" is, what would you say?*

People define it in lots of different ways! But one thing that we can all agree on is that what Paul says in the next section of 1 Corinthians is at the heart of it.

**Read 1 Corinthians 15:1-11**

❓ *How do the Corinthians know the gospel (v 1)?*

❓ *How does Paul know the gospel (v 3)?*

❓ *What does the gospel do (v 2)?*

Here's the gospel in miniature: *"... that Christ died for our sins according to the Scriptures, that he was buried, that he was raised on the third day according to the Scriptures, and that he appeared..."* (v 3-5). This defines the essence of the Christian message: the death of Jesus Christ for our sins. It insists that this was all to fulfill Scripture, and describes Jesus as the Christ, the Messiah, the King of Israel. It includes his burial as an element of Christian proclamation, which is important when you meet someone who believes that he didn't really die or that his body was eaten by wild animals.

❓ *Think about what you would say to someone if you were to explain the gospel—or what you have said in the past. Would you miss any of these things out? Why is each one important?*

## Eyewitnesses

❓ *Who did Jesus appear to after he was raised (v 5-8)?*

❓ *Why do you think Paul makes a point of listing all these people?*

Paul saw the risen Christ himself on the road to Damascus, but because it was after the ascension, and a while after the other apostles saw Christ, he regards himself as "one abnormally born" (v 8).

❓ *Why does Paul call himself the "least of the apostles" (v 9)?*

❓ *But why does this not matter anymore (v 11)?*

As Paul concludes his summary of the gospel, he cannot help but point the Corinthians back to the grace of God at work in his own life (v 10).

❓ *What would be the equivalent for you—how have you seen God's grace at work in your own life?*

❓ *How would you use that as part of your own gospel explanation?*

## ⌃ Pray

List a few friends with whom you would love to share the gospel. Write out some words you might say to them about Jesus. Pray for an opportunity to actually say those words—and that your friends would receive them as truth.

# Foundation truth

*What do you think people find it hardest to believe in—the resurrection of Jesus or the afterlife more generally?*

I'm guessing your answer to that question is the resurrection of Jesus. Lots of people believe in some kind of afterlife—although it might not be the bodily resurrection and new creation of Christian belief. But they have a harder time believing in the resurrection of Jesus.

But it seems it was the opposite in Paul's time. Some people in Corinth believed in Christ's resurrection, but no longer held to the future resurrection of believers. But Paul wants to make it clear that you cannot believe in one without the other.

❷ *Why do you think it is important to believe in Jesus' resurrection?*
❷ *How did Paul know that Jesus had been raised from the dead (see verse 8)?*

## How can you say...?
**Read 1 Corinthians 15:12-20**

❷ *What's Paul's first problem with the Corinthians' belief (v 13)?*
❷ *What's his second problem (v 14)?*
❷ *What's the third problem (v 15)?*
❷ *What's the fourth problem (v 17-19)?*

The stakes could not be higher. If there is no resurrection, then Christians are the most pitiable people on the face of the earth!

## A total crash

It is fascinating how much would unravel for Paul if the resurrection of Jesus were not true. If the corpse of Jesus had been found somewhere, it would not just mean that the walls of Christianity needed repointing; it would mean the entire house had come crashing down. If Jesus is still dead, then sins have not been forgiven and Christians are all lost, hopeless liars.

"But Christ has indeed been raised from the dead" (v 20).

## Pray

Look back at what Paul has said in verses 13-19. He uses a series of "if ... then" phrases. They are all negative. Below are positive versions of these phrases. Fill in the rest of each sentence, showing what the truth is about the resurrection and its implications.

*Since there is a resurrection from the dead (v 13)...*

*Since Christ has been raised (v 14-15)...*

*Since Christ has been raised (v 17-18)...*

*Since we have hope in Christ for the next life as well as this one (v 19)...*

Now turn these sentences into prayers of thanksgiving!

# The death of death

*Paul's next statements have brought hope to billions of grieving and suffering Christians for 20 centuries.*

**Read 1 Corinthians 15:20-34**

Firstfruits were the first part of the crop (of wheat, olive oil, grapes or whatever) to emerge every year, and they were given as an offering to God—but they were also celebrated, because they served as a guarantee that the rest of the crop was coming.

Christ's resurrection is like this. Because he has burst forth into life, you can know for certain that it is only a matter of time before all his people do too.

## Who's in?

Verses 21-23 say that we are either "in" Adam (because of our shared humanity) or "in" Christ (through our faith in him). Death came through Adam, so, naturally, all humans die. But if we are in Christ, through whom resurrection came, we will be made alive.

But everything happens in order. Christ rises first, and *then* "those who belong to him" (v 23). The present age is a period of waiting.

## ✔ Apply

- ❷ *How often do you think about your own resurrection? How do you feel about it?*
- ❷ *How does the image of firstfruits help us to wait for our own resurrection with the right attitude?*

## The end

Waiting for our resurrection can be hard, especially in times of suffering. but there is a reason for the delay.

- ❷ *What else are we waiting for (v 24-25)?*
- ❷ *How does death fit into this (v 26)?*

In verses 27-28, to avoid misunderstanding, Paul clarifies what he means by "everything" being put under Christ's feet. It doesn't include God the Father. Ultimately, God will be all in all.

## Making sense

Verse 29 may seem bizarre. Paul is not endorsing the practice of baptising people for the dead but rather taking something that the Corinthians are known to be doing and pointing out that it makes no sense if there is no resurrection.

- ❷ *What else doesn't make sense without the resurrection (v 30-32)?*
- ❷ *What do you think is the link between the resurrection and Paul's instruction to "stop sinning" (v 34)?*

## ✔ Apply

- ❷ *What in your own life wouldn't make sense without the resurrection?*
- ❷ *Is there anything you think you should change in your life, as a result of what Paul says here?*

*Bible in a year: Genesis 46-48 • Romans 15:14-33*

# Glory is coming

*But what will the resurrection actually be like? It's a question we've all asked.*

It's a question the Corinthians were asking, too—but not in good faith. Paul's response to their question, "How are the dead raised? With what kind of body will they come?" (v 35) is fairly robust: "How foolish!" (v 36). His tone makes it likely that they were not enquiring genuinely, but mocking the idea of the future resurrection as absurd: *What kind of idiot believes you can live for ever in a body? Bodies age, and decay, and die, and eventually rot. So how on earth is that supposed to work?* It is this sneering, snarky scepticism that Paul regards as foolish.

## A fuller answer

**Read 1 Corinthians 15:35-49**

- ❓ *What are the differences between a seed and a wheat plant?*
- ❓ *If our earthly bodies are like the seed (v 37), what does that imply about our resurrection bodies?*
- ❓ *What other kinds of "body" does Paul mention in verses 39-41? What are the differences between all these things?*

Given the variety of the things God has created, the idea of a resurrection body that is different to our earthly bodies should be no problem at all.

- ❓ *What are the differences between our earthly bodies and our future resurrection bodies (v 42-44)?*

## Apply

- ❓ *How does this description of the earthly human body chime with you? Are there particular ways in which you feel perishable, dishonoured or weak?*
- ❓ *How does Paul's description of your heavenly body change your attitude towards your body now?*

## Spiritual bodies

- ❓ *The first man, Adam, was given life. But what's the difference with the "last Adam", Jesus (v 45)?*
- ❓ *What's the other difference between Adam and Jesus (v 47)?*
- ❓ *Why are these distinctions relevant to us (v 48-49)?*

Our heavenly bodies will be modelled on Jesus' body, not on Adam's. When I consider the resurrection body of Jesus—his transformed physicality, whereby he could appear in a locked room and would never die, but could still hug his friends and enjoy a barbecue on the beach—I start to get quite excited about that!

## Pray

Using Paul's descriptions of the resurrection body, spend some time imagining what the resurrection will be like. Then praise God for this amazing promise!

# The last trumpet

*We have reached the dramatic climax of 1 Corinthians.*

**Read 1 Corinthians 15:50-58**

❓ *Read these verses aloud, as if you were performing them. Which part feels most dramatic or significant? Which phrases jump out at you?*

## Becoming imperishable

When Paul says that flesh and blood cannot inherit the kingdom (v 50), he is not denying that the kingdom is physical. He is denying that it is fleshly. The world to come will not involve decay or death like our current bodies do.

❓ *If the perishable cannot inherit the imperishable (v 50), how can we get to be part of the kingdom of God (v 51-52)?*
❓ *Do we have to die in order for this to happen (v 51)?*
❓ *What will the change be like (v 53)?*

## New clothes

It's worth reflecting on the two very ordinary images that Paul uses here: sleeping and clothing. The early Christians often spoke about death as "falling asleep"—an image which points forward to a day when we will wake up and rise, bodies and all. The clothing image is hugely insightful. Our future resurrection is like trading a set of moth-eaten, mouldy clothes for a brand new outfit that will never perish or degrade. And that means that when we take off these flesh-and-blood clothes in death, we are not doing it in order to walk around naked for ever (without a body), but to put on clothes that last for ever (a resurrection body).

## The victory of God

In verse 56, death is pictured as an insect while sin is the sting. Sin results from spiritual death (see Romans 5)—just as death results from sin (Romans 6). The only way this vicious cycle can be broken is through the victory of God, fulfilling the law and destroying both sin and death at once—which, in the Lord Jesus Christ, is exactly what has happened.

## ⌃ Pray

Who do you know who needs to hear this message that Jesus has victory over death? Pray for them now.

## ⌄ Apply

Without hope in the resurrection, there was always the possibility that the Corinthians had "believed in vain" (1 Corinthians 15:2). But now Paul assures them that their faith is "not in vain" (v 58), because they will indeed be raised.

❓ *What does he urge them to do, therefore?*
❓ *How can you yourself put these things into practice?*

# A gift for God's people

*What would you regard as the essential elements of a biblical church service?*

Given all we've read in 1 Corinthians so far, we might say singing, communion, preaching, prayer, or the exercise of spiritual gifts.

But there's one more thing which Paul seems to regard as crucial.

**Read 1 Corinthians 16:1-4**

❷ *What does Paul tell his readers to do on Sundays (v 1-2)?*
❷ *What will happen then (v 3-4)?*
❷ *Who is the collection for (v 1, 3)?*

## The fourth essential

Four and a half centuries ago, the Heidelberg Catechism defined a church service as containing four things: learning what God's word teaches, participating in the sacraments, praying publicly, and making offerings for the poor. It would be interesting to know how many contemporary churches would agree that generosity is so fundamental!

This collection for poor Christians in Jerusalem was not a one-off. Paul had already told the Galatian churches to do the same thing (v 1), and his letters are filled with similar references. He also urges the Romans to give to "the poor among the Lord's people in Jerusalem" (Romans 15:26); elsewhere he encourages his readers to give to widows and poor family members (1 Timothy 5:3, 8). The Philippians gave Paul himself money when he was in need (Philippians 4:14-18).

❷ *Who do you think Paul would want us to give money to today?*

## Generosity guidelines

Paul does not just urge generosity. He also teaches us *how* to give.

First, he shows the priority of giving. It is something you should do at the start of the week, not as an afterthought at the end of the month. For many of us today, that will mean giving by standing order at the start of each month.

Second, he teaches the necessity of giving. It's not just for the rich. "Each one of you" should give (1 Corinthians 16:2).

Third, we see the proportionality of giving: the amount we give should be in keeping with the amount we have (v 2).

Fourth, Paul's instructions here display the practicality of giving. It has to be planned and done properly.

## Pray

Spend some time praying about your own finances. Ask God to lead you in answering the following questions:

❷ *Who or what should I give to?*
❷ *How much should I give?*
❷ *How and when should I give?*

*Bible in a year: Isaiah 3-4 • Mark 1:23-45*

# The greatest and least

*David has already said at the start of this psalm that he called to the Lord for rescue, and God saved him. He now describes how.*

## A God of action

**Read Psalm 18:7-19**

The language with which God is described is terrifying. He is the earthquake (v 7); he is the volcano (v 8); he is the raging storm (v 12); he is the thunder and lightning (v 14); he is the hurricane (v 15). David trawls the world for the most appalling images of the destructive forces of nature, and weaves them into this description of what it would be like to come face to face with the living God. The point is this: if God was able to do these things, then he is certainly able to save, provide and protect us now and in the future. And this terrifying God breaks into the world he made with the express purpose of saving this one weak, insignificant human being.

> ❓ *Why does he do that (v 19)?*

## A God of justice

**Read Psalm 18:20-29**

> ❓ *How does God deal with people (v 20-21)?*

Since we often yearn for justice in an unjust world, this is great news. But since our hands are often not clean, it is only great news because (as we saw in Psalm 15) it's Jesus' perfection, not ours, which we rely on, and then seek to imitate.

## ⌃ Pray

The gospel is not fair. Fairness would have us all facing the tempestuously angry God with our sins unforgiven. It is unfair that some should receive heaven through what Christ has done. The God of the Bible is partisan. He takes sides. He delights in those who are clean in his sight (v 24). The word for this is grace.

Pause for a while to give thanks that you're loved and rescued.

## A God of victory

**Read Psalm 18:30-50**

Verse 50 points us to the ultimate victor—to the promised descendant of David, the Lord Jesus. We can sing of what God has done in our lives—but most of all, we will want to sing of what God has done for us in Jesus' life.

## ⌃ Pray

The awesome God who David loved is the God every Christian knows.

Praise him for saving you through Christ Jesus. Use the words of verses 30-36 and 46-50 in a time of thanks and praise.

# Plans and people

*The closing greetings of Paul's letters remind us of something crucial—that he was writing to specific people in a specific time and place.*

**Read 1 Corinthians 16:5-11**

Paul is writing from Ephesus, on the west coast of what is now Turkey, in the spring of either AD 54 or 55.

- ❓ *What's his immediate-term plan (v 8)?*
- ❓ *Why (v 9)?*
- ❓ *What does he hope to do after that (v 5-7)?*
- ❓ *What kind of visit does he want to make to the Corinthians (v 7)?*
- ❓ *In the meantime, he's sending Timothy—to do what (v 10)?*

## Face time

Paul wants genuine relationship, not a fly-by or a whistle-stop tour. Travelling preachers should take note!

His overriding motivation is to do the work of the Lord. That's why he's staying in Ephesus. But he wants God's work to continue in Corinth, too—so he is sending Timothy to visit them and see how they are.

- ❓ *Why do you think Paul felt that long visits and face-to-face time are so crucial?*

## 🔽 Apply

- ❓ *Does this challenge the way you think about your relationships with Christian friends or family who live far away?*

- ❓ *In what ways do you think you could use the time you spend face-to-face with other Christians to do God's work among them?*

## Room to change

Notice how provisional Paul is in his plans: "Perhaps"; "wherever I go" (v 6); "I hope … if the Lord permits" (v 7). Paul has travelled enough, and followed the leading (and sometimes the obstructing—see Acts 16:6-10!) of the Spirit enough, to know that things do not always work out the way that we think they will. So he is happy to disclose his plans, as long as people know that God in his sovereignty may see fit to change them. We would do well to imitate him when we make our own plans for the future.

## 🔼 Pray

- ❓ *What future plans are you making? How can you hold them loosely?*
- ❓ *What friends do you long to see? How would you love to see God working in and among them?*
- ❓ *Do you have any friends (maybe ones who have fallen off your radar) whom you could encourage and help with some face-to-face time?*

Pray that God will align your priorities with his priorities as you plan your social life and seek to serve those around you.

# All together now

*How do you feel about those you serve alongside at church? What about people from churches that do things differently to yours?*

There are plenty of church committees, teams, and councils where people work with each other but don't seem to like each other very much.

But the end of Paul's letter to the Corinthians—as with so many of his letters—displays the warmth and genuineness of relationship that unites Paul and his ministry partners, and the churches they serve.

## Brothers and sisters

### Read 1 Corinthians 16:10-24

- ❓ *How does Paul show his concern for Timothy (v 10-11)?*
- ❓ *Apollos doesn't seem to be cooperating with Paul's plans. But how does Paul describe him (v 12)?*
- ❓ *What four things does Paul appreciate about Stephanas and his household (v 15-18; Fortunatus and Achaicus were probably either Stephanas' slaves or his adult sons)?*
- ❓ *How does he want the Corinthians to treat them, therefore (v 15-16, 18)?*

## Be ready

In the middle of these statements comes an unexpected list of five instructions that should characterise the Corinthians' behaviour (v 13-14).

The first four remind us that, for Paul, the Christian life is a battle, filled with dangers

and requiring constant vigilance. But the fifth is different. "Do everything in love." The first four without the fifth will lead to disaster.

It's this love that Paul is showing throughout his statements in this chapter.

## Warm greetings

Churches do not just have relationships with other people; we have relationships with other churches. That truth comes to the fore in verses 19-20. The Corinthian church is much loved, not only by people who established it (like Paul) or who used to belong to it (like Aquila and Priscilla) but by hundreds of believers who have never been to Corinth and never will. All are part of the body of Christ, and that means interconnectedness and mutual love.

## The sign-off

- ❓ *In his final greetings, how does Paul show where all this love comes from?*

## ⌄ Apply

- ❓ *How can you show grace and love to those in your church?*
- ❓ *How can you show grace and love to those in other churches?*
- ❓ *How else can you celebrate your unity with other Christians in Christ this week?*

*Bible in a year: Isaiah 10-13 • Mark 4:1-20*

# ISAIAH:
# A book of good news

Isaiah can seem somewhat intimidating. It's a big book covering an extended timescale, full of unfamiliar names and places. But it's a book full of good news, and it's news worth shouting about. All the time it is pointing forward to Jesus.

NOTE: These studies won't cover every verse of Isaiah. Instead we are going to focus on representative passages which will help us see the overall message of the book.

## A rebellious nation

Isaiah ministered about 800 years before Christ. In the next two studies we'll focus on chapter 6, which begins "In the year that King Uzziah died": 739 BC. That chapter is often known as Isaiah's call, although his ministry probably started before this event, during the reign of Uzziah.

**Read Isaiah 1:1-4**

❓ *What does Isaiah say his vision is going to be about (v 1)?*
❓ *What kind of relationship does God want to have with his people (v 2-3)?*
❓ *But what have they done (v 3-4)?*

The first five chapters of Isaiah function as a kind of "overture". They preview some of the key themes in the rest of the book.

Isaiah condemns God's people for their rebellion against God and their injustice to-wards one another. He promises a glorious future for Jerusalem, but contrasts that with the present reality of her sin. The long-term future may be glorious, but the immediate future contains judgment.

## A beloved vineyard

In chapter 5, Isaiah sings a song in which God's people are compared to a vineyard.

**Read Isaiah 5:1-7**

❓ *How does the owner of the vineyard care for it (v 2)?*
❓ *How has it responded to his care (v 2, 4)?*
❓ *So what will the owner do (v 5-6)?*

The comparison becomes explicit in verse 7.

❓ *What "bad fruit" have God's people borne (v 7)?*
❓ *Do you think God is right to respond as he does?*

## 🔺 Pray

The key to unlocking the treasures in Isaiah is to tremble at God's word (33:6). We're to come with a humble and contrite spirit (66:2), ready to be confronted about with our sin and injustice. But we can also expect a rich store of wisdom and an experience of his favour.

❓ *In today's passages, what is God like?*
❓ *What does he care about?*

Spend some time praising him for who he is, and committing yourself to him as you read Isaiah.

# Holy, holy, holy

*We sometimes assume God is like us, but bigger. That's the wrong way round! We only discover the truth about ourselves when we truly see God.*

Isaiah 6 describes a vision of God that became the defining perspective of Isaiah's life and ministry.

**Read Isaiah 6:1-5**

- ❷ *Look at the way God is described in verse 1. What does this show about him?*
- ❷ *What about the song in verse 3? What does this tell us about God?*
- ❷ *Why do you think there is shaking and smoke in verse 4? What impression does it give of God?*

Seraphim are angelic beings, made by God to attend him in his heavenly court. These are beings which have never sinned. But they don't possess the holiness and purity that God possesses. So they have to cover their eyes and feet in God's presence.

Isaiah sees the holiness of God in the seraphim's wings; he hears the holiness of God in their cry; he feels the holiness of God as the doorposts shake; and he smells the holiness of God as smoke fills the temple.

## A consuming fire

God's holiness is not so much an attribute of God as it is the perfection and intensity of all his other attributes. God's holiness is the perfection of his love, power, purity, wisdom and justice. He is perfect love and purest purity. He has the wisest strength and the strongest wisdom. The Bible describes God as a consuming fire. Think of the white-hot

heat of a bonfire. You can't take your eyes off it, and yet you feel its danger. Our God is a consuming fire, burning with the intensity of his holiness like the burning centre of a star. Anything tainted by sin is consumed in the presence of his powerful purity and perfect love.

- ❷ *How does Isaiah respond to this holiness? Why?*

The holiness of God is a threat to sinful people. The phrase "I am ruined" (v 5) is literally "I'm destroyed" or even "I'm disintegrating". God's holiness presses in on Isaiah, and he feels crushed. A friend once said of someone we both knew, "If he realised the impact of his actions on other people, it would crush him". In reality that's true of us all. It's only before God that we attain true self-knowledge—and it's devastating.

## ⌄ Apply

- ❷ *What's your view of yourself, generally? How do you usually describe yourself?*
- ❷ *When you imagine yourself in Isaiah's shoes, standing before a holy God, does your view of yourself change?*

## A burning coal

**Read Isaiah 6:6-7**

God can take away our guilt. Confess your sin and know that, if you trust in Christ, then your sin, too, has been atoned for.

# Here am I

*When you've seen the majesty of God and when you've experienced his grace, you cannot help but want to serve him.*

### Read Isaiah 6:8-13

Isaiah has just said, "I am a man of unclean lips" (v 5)! But when he hears God saying, "Whom shall I send?" he responds, "Here am I. Send me!" He's not saying, *I'll do you a favour* or *I'm the ideal man for the job.* He wants to serve.

❓ *What job does Isaiah get (v 9-10)?*
❓ *Do you think this is what he was expecting?*

Isaiah is going to speak to people who will refuse to listen! And God is going to use him to harden their hearts, confirm their blindness and prepare them for judgment.

···· TIME OUT ·······················

This isn't unique to Isaiah. Jesus quoted Isaiah 6 to explain why he spoke in parables (Matthew 13:10-17). John's Gospel quotes Isaiah 6:10 to explain why even those who encountered Jesus were blind to his glory (John 12:37-41).

Left to ourselves, none of us would seek God. We are deaf to his voice and blind to his glory. But when the Holy Spirit opens our ears and eyes, we recognise the glory of God in the face of Jesus Christ.

## How long?

❓ *What will happen as a result of the people's deafness (Isaiah 6:11-12)?*

❓ *But what does God promise will be left in the land (v 13)?*

Israel and Judah (the two kingdoms of God's people) will be defeated and exiled. But in the wastes of judgment, there will be something left that is alive—even if only just.

So it is that later, in Isaiah 52:15, we read, "For what they were not told, they will see, and what they have not heard, they will understand". It's the exact opposite of 6:9. Isaiah would encounter people who had heard but did not understand. But one day there would be people who had not heard but did understand.

❓ *How do you think Isaiah might have felt as the Lord told him what would happen?*

## ☑ Apply

❓ *In what ways do you seek to serve the Lord?*
❓ *How could you serve God with your words, in particular?*

God uses us in the same way he used Isaiah. To some, our words bring life. But other people reject our words, and, in doing so, they're confirmed in their judgment—both their judgment against Christ and God's judgment against them.

In God's grace, he sought us out. Let's pray that he would open the eyes of those around us, too.

# Hearts are shaken

*What's the biggest threat we face at the moment? Climate change? The fallout of a global pandemic? Or more personal issues? For many people the future feels gloomy.*

In Isaiah 7, the future also looked gloomy for God's people. After the death of King Solomon in 931BC the nation had divided into two: Judah in the south, and Israel, also known as Ephraim, in the north. In Isaiah 7, the king of Judah is Ahaz, and he has a problem. Ephraim has ganged up with another nation, Aram, against Judah.

### Read Isaiah 7:1-9

> ❓ *How does Ahaz feel (v 2)?*
> ❓ *But how does God encourage him to feel (v 4)?*
> ❓ *Why?*

## An unwanted sign
### Read Isaiah 7:10-17

Isaiah invites Ahaz to ask for a sign (v 10-11). He says, in effect, *Let God reassure you*. But Ahaz refuses. Basically he is saying, *Thanks, but no thanks*. He's going to look for help elsewhere.

So God gives Ahaz a sign that he's not looking for.

> ❓ *What is the sign (v 14)?*
> ❓ *What else does God promise (v 16-17)?*

We know verse 14 as a famous Christmas promise. But originally it was a word of judgment. Ahaz is a descendant of King David. God had promised David that his line would always rule over God's people. So Ahaz thinks God needs him in order to keep his promise. But here God is saying,

*I can bring the reign of David's godless sons to an end and then start again with a virgin.* Ahaz thinks he can do without God, but it's God who can do without Ahaz.

## A scary promise

The promised boy will grow up eating honey and curds (v 15). It's the food of poverty—a sign that Judah's economy will collapse. So Jesus will come, and he will be called "Immanuel": God with us. But before this happens, Judah will have experienced defeat and exile.

Yes, God will defeat Ephraim and Aram (v 16). He will call the Assyrians to defeat these two nations. But these "floodwaters" will sweep over Judah as well (8:5-8).

## ⌄ Apply

God has given us a sign, too: his name is Immanuel. When Jesus came to earth, he showed us our sin and warned us of judgment, but he also reassured us of God's presence and gave us a way to be saved.

> ❓ *What do you fear? What would it look like for you to do as God tells Ahaz and be calm and trustful?*
> ❓ *In what areas of life are you tempted to do without God? Or in what ways do you fall into the trap of thinking God needs you? How can you be more honest with yourself about your need for God?*

# Signs in the sky

*"If only God would make himself known!" How often has someone (perhaps you yourself) said or thought something like this?*

In Psalm 19, David describes two "books" that speak about the nature and character of God—the sky and the Scriptures. The first is described in verses 1-6— the second, we'll think about next week.

## Speech without words

**Read Psalm 19:1-2**

- ❓ *What do the heavens do?*
- ❓ *What do they tell us:*
  - *about who God is?*
  - *about his relationship to the universe?*

## A blaring sermon

**Read Psalm 19:3-6**

- ❓ *Where do the heavens speak?*
- ❓ *What part of earth is left without this witness (v 6)?*
- ❓ *Who has a good excuse for not knowing that there is a Creator God?*

The sky is like a wordless language that speaks to all people (v 3). It talks to mankind all night long and everybody hears it (v 4). During the day, the magnificent life-giving, regular-as-clockwork sun does the same thing. "The Creator is amazing and faithful" they both cry.

## ✔ Apply

The skill of a handyman cannot be known apart from his handiwork. To miss the product is to miss the producer.

So look regularly at the sky and sun today. And praise God each time. The heavens exist to point to God's glory. So does everything God created—and that includes us and other people. When you see others today, let your first thought be to praise God for the wonderful way he has made them.

---- TIME OUT ......................

- ❓ *If the heavens are so clear about God, why do people not listen to this insistent sermon?*

**Read Romans 1:18-21**

No one is ignorant of the truth, except through their own self-deception and wilful disobedience.

Everyone is ultimately culpable, because the infinite wonder of the skies speaks plainly to everyone in a universal language. But even so, there is more to know, more that is knowable about God.

But for that, we'll need next week's "book".

# Darkness and light

*We've seen King Ahaz's response to his nation's gloomy outlook. But how else did people respond?*

### Read Isaiah 8:19-22

- ❓ *Who are people going to for guidance and reassurance (v 19)?*
- ❓ *Why do you think they are not going to God (v 19-20)?*
- ❓ *What is their attitude towards God (v 21)?*
- ❓ *What's the result of all this?*

The people see only gloom. That's what happens when you take God out of the picture. If you take God away, you take justice away with him; for without God, there are no objective criteria to judge what is right and wrong. There's no one to hold people to account. There's no light of revelation and no hope of redemption.

If humanity is left to itself, it is not a happy prospect. Without God, the best we can hope for is to muddle through life without facing a major illness, crime, redundancy or war. But even if people avoid these things, in the end every life ends in death.

But into this distress, darkness and gloom, light is coming.

## A light has dawned

### Read Isaiah 9:1-2

Zebulun and Naphtali were the two most northerly of the twelve tribes of Israel. So when the Assyrian army came, it came first to Zebulun and Naphtali. The darkness fell on them first.

These regions were already notorious as areas in which the first generation of Israelites in the land had failed to drive out the Canaanites (Judges 1:30, 33). Galilee, too, had a dubious reputation. Solomon gave 20 Galilean towns to Hiram king of Tyre in return for building supplies, but it seems Hiram had been somewhat underwhelmed by what he had received. He nicknamed them "the Land of Kabul" which means "good-for-nothing", a name which the writer of Kings says "they have to this day" (1 Kings 9:10-13). No wonder Isaiah says they were humbled.

But that was "in the past". Now Isaiah contrasts their past with what will happen "in the future". The promise is that a light is coming, and it's going to come to them first. The distress, darkness and gloom with which we ended chapter 8 are going to give way to light.

## ⌃ Pray

Who do you know who is "walking in darkness"? Perhaps they are enduring suffering or uncertainty. Perhaps they have rejected God. Spend some time praying for the light of hope and revelation to come in their lives.

HOPE|EXPLORED

WHAT'S THE BEST FUTURE
YOU COULD EVER IMAGINE?

# NEW THREE-WEEK EVANGELISTIC COURSE

*Hope Explored* is a video-based evangelistic course from Christianity Explored Ministries looking at the life, death, and resurrection of Jesus in Luke's Gospel over just three sessions.

To run the course, customers will need a Leader's Handbook, Handbooks for each participant and the videos—either a DVD or digital downloads. Can be run in person or on video-meeting technology, in small groups or one-to-one.

**thegoodbook.co.uk/hope-explored**
**thegoodbook.com/hope-explored**

# To us a child is born

*Light will come—but how?*

**Read Isaiah 9:1-7**

❓ *How many times does Isaiah talk about joy (v 3)?*

❓ *What is God going to put an end to (v 4-5)?*

It's easy to see what an amazing promise this is. It's unbelievably good news. But how will it happen?

Verse 6 begins "For". Here's the means by which God will end oppression and war: a child.

This is the son promised in Isaiah 7:14 and the son promised to David in 2 Samuel 7:12-14. A new king is coming, who will reign over God's people in justice and peace. This is Jesus.

···· **TIME OUT** ································

**Read Luke 1:31-33**

❓ *How many connections can you find between what the angel says to Mary and what Isaiah says in 9:6-7?*

Matthew 4:14-16 also quotes from Isaiah 9:1 to show that this promise is fulfilled by Jesus. The early ministry of Jesus took place in Galilee, where Isaiah said the light would dawn. Jesus is the one who ends our fear and dispels our gloom.

································

❓ *What political language can you see in Isaiah 9:6-7?*

We're not to over-spiritualise this—it's a political message. It's the promise of a new and better government. One day Jesus will return and establish his government, "upholding it with justice and righteousness from that time on and for ever".

## He will be called...

"Wonderful Counsellor" is the language of "signs and wonders". It means Jesus has miraculous or supernatural wisdom.

Isaiah promises a human child—but he calls him "Mighty God". God himself, in the person of Jesus, has entered our world.

"Everlasting Father" also looks odd, especially as the coming king has just been called a "child" and a "son". But it echoes Isaiah 1:2. God has been a father to his people. He created them and cared for them. Now he is coming to recreate his people.

"Prince of peace" points to the fact that God will defeat his people's enemies and bring peace. But Jesus also brings peace with God. We saw in 6:5 and 7:17 that God is the real threat to sinful people. But Jesus makes peace with God on our behalf.

## 🔼 Pray

Which part of this description of Jesus is most helpful for you today? How does it help you to trust him? Praise God for sending his Son to us!

*Bible in a year: Isaiah 30-31 • Mark 7:14-37*

# God's righteous anger

*The remainder of Isaiah 9 is a sobering chapter.*

❓ *Where and when have you seen arrogance, bad leadership, exploitation, or oppression?*
❓ *How did you feel about these things?*
❓ *Were you able to do anything about them? What would you have liked to do?*

## Judgment comes
### Read Isaiah 9:8-21

Arrogance, bad leadership, exploitation and oppression is what Isaiah saw in the northern kingdom, Israel, and he describes it in 9:8 – 10:4. Repeatedly, he tells us how God will respond: "His anger is not turned away, his hand is still upraised" (9:12).

• In verses 8-12 Israel think they can rebuild, instead they're going to be devoured. But God's anger is still not turned away.

• In verses 13-17 God will take away their leaders and prophets because everyone is ungodly. But even this will not be enough.

• In verses 18-21 the people will be consumed both by the fires of their own wickedness and by the fire of God's anger.

• In 10:1-4 Isaiah says that, because of their injustice, there will be nowhere to hide when God judges.

The up-raised hand of God in Isaiah 9 – 10 is not the end of the story! But for now, God's "hand is still upraised" (10:4).

## A tool in God's hand

Isaiah is describing how God is going to use the Assyrian Empire to judge Israel—and then Judah (v 21). Next he turns his attention to Assyria itself.

### Read Isaiah 10:12-19

❓ *What claim does the king of Assyria make (v 13-14)?*
❓ *But how does God put him in his place (v 15)?*
❓ *What will happen to Assyria (v 16-19)?*

Assyria is a tool being used by God. But the motives of the Assyrians are far from good (10:7). So God will judge Assyria, too.

## Pray

❓ *Where around you do you see injustice, arrogance and bad leadership?*

Use some of the words from Isaiah 9:8 – 10:19 to pray that God would bring justice and righteousness to this world.

❓ *Where in yourself do you see unjust attitudes, arrogance and wrong motives?*

Confess your sins to God and ask for his mercy and help to change.

# A green shoot

*We need to pause at this point and take in the scene.*

As far as the eye can see there's just blackened earth. Israel, Judah and Assyria are all subject to God's judgment. In 10:33 Isaiah likens God to a lumberjack as he describes Assyria's defeat:

*"See, the Lord, the LORD Almighty,*
*will lop off the boughs with great power.*
*The lofty trees will be felled,*
*the tall ones will be brought low."*

But then Isaiah sees something in the ruin, the death and the emptiness.

**Read Isaiah 11:1-9**

❷ *What's the connection in verse 1 with the devastation we saw in 10:33?*

The stump of Jesse is the family of David, Israel's greatest king. So this is a promise of a new David coming.

❷ *What will the Spirit equip this new king with (v 2)?*
❷ *What words describe what this king will be like (v 3-5)?*
❷ *What will the world be like under his rule (v 6-9)?*

## ✓ Apply

This describes Jesus. He was anointed with the Holy Spirit at his baptism, and conducted his ministry with wisdom, understanding, counsel and might. Through the Spirit, Jesus continues to turn his commitment to justice into reality.

Think what that means for the reign of Jesus over your life. He understands you better than you understand yourself. He never puts a foot wrong or speaks a word out of place as he counsels you. As you read his word or hear it preached, Jesus himself is shaping your life with perfect, Spirit-enabled wisdom.

❷ *How will that shape the way you listen to, and your excitement about, God's word?*

## A kingdom of peace

It is difficult to know whether the description in verses 6-9 is literal or symbolic. But the point is clear: under the reign of Jesus, hostilities will end. His kingdom will be a kingdom of peace. Isaiah is describing the coming of Jesus as the restoration of the Garden of Eden. These verses pick up the feeling of Genesis 1:28, where God told Adam and Eve to "be fruitful", to "fill the earth and subdue it", and to rule over the animals. Jesus puts that mandate back on track.

## ⌃ Pray

One day, "the earth will be filled with the knowledge of the LORD as the waters cover the sea". Pray for our world in the light of that promise. Ask Jesus to make his kingdom come on earth. Pray this for yourself and your local community, too.

*Bible in a year: Isaiah 34-36 • Mark 9:1-29* ✓

# Bubbling over

*When it comes to evangelism, I want to be like a champagne bottle—which goes off with a bang, letting the champagne pour and fizz and bubble everywhere.*

Instead I'm often like a tube of toothpaste: I roll myself up with guilt until a tiny bit of Jesus squeezes out.

Isaiah is more like the champagne bottle. He has seen such a wonderful vision of God's coming salvation that, in the next section, he is left fizzing with praise to God—praise that bubbles out to the nations.

**Read Isaiah 11:10-16**

❓ *Who's included in Jesus' glorious reign (v 10, 12)?*

Isaiah describes a repeat of the exodus out of Egypt (v 15-16): the sea will dry up and people will cross it and come home. But this time he is going to create a highway through both the Egyptian Sea and the Euphrates River. These were the two great bodies of water to the south and to the north of Israel. The point is that God's people are going to come home from every direction.

But it's not just Israelites. "He will raise a banner for the nations" (v 12). Verse 11 is a list of nations from every direction—the extent of Isaiah's known world.

## A banner to the world

Jesus has raised a banner so everyone can rally to him. And that banner is us! That is what we are doing in the mission of the church. We hold up the gospel so that everyone whom God has chosen can find their way home.

**Read Isaiah 12:1-6**

❓ *We saw in chapter 9 that God's anger had not turned away. But what has happened to God's anger now (12:1)?*

In 11:4, Isaiah said that when Jesus came, he would "slay the wicked". When did that happen in the ministry of Jesus? It was at the cross. God's judgment fell on Jesus instead of on us. God's anger turned against Jesus instead of against us.

❓ *What will those who have been saved do (12:1-3)?*
❓ *Who will they sing to (v 4-6)?*
❓ *What will they sing about?*

Is Isaiah talking about worship or mission in these verses? Both! Mission is God's people extolling his worth to the nations. If you truly think something is worth worshipping, you tell everyone about it.

## ☑ Apply

❓ *How does all this change the way you think about worship, and about mission?*

Some of us need to spend less time thinking about evangelism and more time thinking about Jesus. We need to spend more time together drawing water from the wells of salvation (v 3). We need to rediscover our enthusiasm for Jesus. Then perhaps we will be like bottles of champagne. When the opportunity comes... Psssh!

❤ *Bible in a year: Isaiah 37-38 • Mark 9:30-50*

# Don't reach for the stars

*We all long to be top of the league, top of the class, top of the tree, best in show. We climb the career ladder or the property ladder. We want to rise.*

Perhaps that's because we know we're *fallen*. We were made in the image of God to reflect his glory in the world, but we rejected God and came tumbling down. And ever since we have tried to scramble back up to the top. But now we do it without God. We want to establish our own glory, not his.

The message of Isaiah 13 – 23 is that this is futile. Human glory is fleeting and temporary.

These chapters are a collection of prophecies addressed to the nations. It begins with a description of the downfall of the Babylonian Empire. 150 years or so after Isaiah's ministry, the Babylonian Empire (in modern-day Iraq) replaced the Assyrians as the regional superpower. The Babylonians destroyed Jerusalem and carried her inhabitants away into exile. But God would defeat Babylon and bring the Jews back to Jerusalem.

## Comeuppance
### Read Isaiah 14:1-23

❓ *How does Isaiah describe the return from exile (v 1-3)?*

Isaiah gives God's people a taunt to sing. He imagines the arrival of the defeated king of Babylon in the realm of the dead.

❓ *How do we see the king's arrogance throughout this passage?*
❓ *What did he do to seek his own glory?*

❓ *But has that glory lasted?*
❓ *What imagery does Isaiah use to help us see the complete reversal in the king's fortunes?*

---- TIME OUT ----

The book of Daniel describes what happened when Babylon fell and Isaiah's prophecy came true.
### Read Daniel 5:18-23, 30-31

Daniel uses the example of a previous king, Nebuchadnezzar, to warn the current king, Belshazzar.

❓ *In what ways have both these kings sought their own glory?*
❓ *How do we see Isaiah's prophecy come true in their lives?*

## ⌄ Apply

❓ *In what areas of life are you most tempted to climb ladders or be the best? In what ways do you long to be impressive?*

We so easily get sucked into thinking human glory and status are what matters. But none of it lasts. However impressive we seem, we will one day face death. But God is sovereign over all nations and all people. We need to recognise God's glory instead.

❓ *What impact will this have on how you think about your answer to the previous question?*

# Signs on the page

*Last week we thought about the wordless sermon that creation preaches to everyone on earth: God is amazing, wonderful and faithful. But where do we find more detail?*

## Speaking clearly

- ❷ *If someone just had creation to go by, what picture of God might they come up with?*
- ❷ *What questions would it leave unanswered?*
- ❷ *How do you see these features played out in "natural religion"?*

Paul tells us that we can discern God's greatness and power from his creation, but to know more, we need a more specific revelation...

**Read Psalm 19:7-11**

- ❷ *Find six characteristics of God's law in these verses and try to put them in your own words.*
- ❷ *How does the world offer substandard versions of each of these things (i.e. what are their opposites)?*

Most of us treat rules as things to be suffered and obeyed (for fear of being caught) with a scowl on our faces. But notice the effect that God's laws should have on us:

- They bring new life to us (v 7a).
- They make us live more intelligently (v 7b).
- They make us truly happy (v 8).
- They help us understand the world (v 8b).
- They keep us safe (v 11).

These are the things that most people desire most out of life; and they are on offer to all through God's word.

## ☑ Apply

Work through this list line by line and search your own heart.

- ❷ *Are you as convinced as David of these truths?*
- ❷ *Do you really think that God's word is sweeter than honey?*
- ❷ *What makes you doubt these truths, and prevents you from embracing them fully?*

Talk to God about your answer...

## Searching the heart

**Read Psalm 19:12-14**

- ❷ *What does reading God's commands make David realise?*
- ❷ *What are the two types of sin in v 12-13?*
- ❷ *Why does he ask for God's help?*
- ❷ *So what should we do right now?*

## Searching the future

David lived with an incomplete revelation of God. The way to serve the Lord was to delight in and be obedient to the law. Temple sacrifices dealt with sin. And yet we discern in David's life and his writing repeated expressions of the gaps in understanding. These questions would only be resolved when God's Word became flesh, and Christ was revealed as the ultimate revelation of who God is and what his purposes are in the world.

# A plan for the nations

*It's not just Babylon. Next Isaiah describes the fate of the Assyrians, and soon he moves on to the Philistines.*

The point is that God is sovereign over all nations. The remainder of Isaiah 13 – 23 makes that abundantly clear.

**Read Isaiah 14:24-32**

> ❷ *What will God do to Assyria (v 24-25)?*
> ❷ *What about to the Philistines (v 29-30)?*

The judgment on Babylon and Assyria is a pointer to the judgment of all humanity. This is why verse 29 says, "Do not rejoice, all you Philistines, that the rod that struck you is broken". Why not? Because Philistia will also be judged by God.

> ❷ *What does Isaiah want us to learn about God (v 27)?*

## All the nations

In the next chapters, Isaiah addresses all the surrounding nations and beyond:

• Moab (15:1 – 16:14)
• Damascus—the capital of Aram (17:1-14)
• Cush—the upper Nile region (18:1-7)
• Egypt—the lower Nile region (19:1-17)
• Egypt and Cush together (20:1-6)
• Babylon (again) (21:1-10)
• Edom—symbolically called Dumah or "silence" (21:11-12)
• Arabia (21:13-17)
• Jerusalem—the capital of Judah (22:1-14)
• Tyre (23:1-18)

These prophecies were spoken to the people of Judah. They show that in reality all the people they fear are under God's control.

## ⌃ Pray

> ❷ *What situations tempt you to doubt God's word?*
> ❷ *How does this passage help you to trust him?*

Spend some time in prayer, acknowledging his lordship over the whole world and over your life.

## Refuge and welcome

> ❷ *In 14:32, where does God say there will be refuge?*

Zion was the hill upon which Jerusalem was built. But Isaiah cannot be talking about physical Jerusalem because in chapter 22 Jerusalem is included in the nations that will be judged. That is why he says "Zion" and not "Jerusalem". He is not talking primarily about the physical return from exile that would happen after the defeat of Babylon. He is talking about those who find refuge in Jesus Christ.

Babylonian exile was a picture of a larger exile—humanity's exile from God. But now the forces of sin and death which enslave us have been overthrown through the death and resurrection of Jesus. And one day God will gather his people from every nation and bring us home.

# Going global

*The Bible says that one day God will judge humanity. It's a truth we often hesitate to mention.*

Perhaps it's true that it will put people off our message. But it's also the case that the world is full of reasons for divine judgment. Spend a few minutes watching the news and you will have a strong sense that something should be done. We want evil to be punished and wrongs to be righted.

## Universal judgment

So far, Isaiah has described judgments which took place in history. But it turns out these are all pointers to a global judgment at the end of history.

### Read Isaiah 24:1-6

- ❓ *How does Isaiah highlight the fact that the coming devastation will be for all people?*
- ❓ *How does he show that it's going to be for the whole earth?*
- ❓ *What is God's reason for this judgment (v 5-6)?*

God had made a covenant with his people, Israel, at Mount Sinai, which they had broken. But Isaiah also takes us back to an older covenant: a covenant as old as time. Creation implies a covenant in which the creature is bound to honour and obey the Creator (Romans 2:14-15). And this covenant has been broken by all humanity. The reason for universal judgment is universal sin.

If you find this vision disturbing, that's because it is meant to shake us from our complacency. The violence of God is terrible to behold. But God's judgment is not arbitrary or indiscriminate. His judgment is the response of his love to the suffering we inflict on one another.

## ⌃ Pray

"People must bear their guilt" (Isaiah 24:6). But later in Isaiah, we will learn of one who has borne our guilt on our behalf (53:6): Jesus.

How seriously do you take your own sin? Acknowledge your guilt before God. Then thank him that in Jesus you have been cleansed of your guilt.

···· TIME OUT ····

### Read 2 Peter 3:10-13

- ❓ *What does Peter say will happen to the earth?*
- ❓ *What's the end of the story (v 13)?*
- ❓ *What should we do in the meantime?*

## In that day
### Read Isaiah 24:19-23

- ❓ *Who and what will remain after the earth has been devastated (v 23)?*

Isaiah doesn't promise that everything will work out the way we'd like. But everything *will* work out to God's glory. We need to see the world from that perspective—that's what will keep our footing secure.

# The great reversal

*What makes you overflow with praise to God?*

**Read Isaiah 25:1-12**

This is a song of praise. But Isaiah is praising God because he has made the city a heap of rubble (v 1-2).

Perhaps this feels counterintuitive. But let me suggest that in fact it is deeply intuitive. How many hundreds of movies have you seen in which the bad guy gets his comeuppance and your heart exults? That's Isaiah's feeling here as he contemplates the day when justice will be done. The phrase "perfect faithfulness" in verse 1 translates two words with the same root. So it literally means something like "faithfully faithful". God will prove faithfully faithful to his promise.

God's justice isn't whimsical or arbitrary. It's not that he sometimes lets people get away with evil and sometimes doesn't. He is faithfully faithful. He will make all things right in the end.

## A patterned song

This is one of three songs in Isaiah 24 – 27 which help us know how to respond to the declarations of devastation. It's in five sections with the first and last sections paralleling each other, the second and penultimate sections paralleling one another, and a core central section, which is the heart of the message.

> ❷ What reversals do we see in Isaiah 25:1-3 and 10-12?

> ❷ What's the theme in verses 4-5 and 9?
> ❷ Which of the images that Isaiah uses in v 4-5 help you understand and apply his message best?
> ❷ How do these four sections reveal God to be "faithfully faithful"?
> ❷ How do you think Isaiah wants us to respond to his prophecy of God's judgment?

## The LORD has spoken

The central section of the song is verses 6-8. Isaiah is describing your future if you're in Christ by faith, and it is a feast. Our emptiness will be filled; our thirsts will be quenched; our needs will be met. More than this, a feast speaks of communion. God invites us to a meal with him. It's a sign that our relationship has been restored.

> ❷ What else does God promise (v 7-8)?

## ⌃ Pray

> ❷ How many reasons to praise God can you find in this passage?

We often praise God for his faithfulness and for saving us, but most of us don't spend much time praising God for his coming judgment.

Spend time praising God for his faithfulness in keeping his promises—including his promise to judge the earth.

# Good fruit at last

*Back in Isaiah 5 the prophet sang of how God nurtured his "vineyard". But it bore only bad fruit. So he let it become a wasteland.*

It is a picture of the way in which God chose Israel to be his people, rescued them from slavery, revealed his glory to them at Mount Sinai and planted them in the promised land. Everything was put in place for them to serve him in love. But instead of doing good works, Israel produced only the bad fruit of evil acts.

In Isaiah 27, God again sings about his vineyard.

## In that day

**Read Isaiah 27:2-6**

- ❷ *How does God treat his vineyard (v 3)?*
- ❷ *How will he deal with weeds (v 4)?*
- ❷ *But what does he really want his people to do (v 5)?*
- ❷ *What will be the result (v 6)?*

Isaiah 5:7 reveals the meaning of the "bad fruit" which Israel previously bore, and the "good fruit" which God desires:

*"He looked for justice, but saw bloodshed; for righteousness, but heard cries of distress".*

Bloodshed and distress: this is the fruit of our evil acts. This is what God is coming to destroy.

- ❷ *How does the image of the vineyard help you to understand why God comes in judgment?*
- ❷ *How does it comfort and assure you of God's good purposes?*

## Bear much fruit

This passage in Isaiah is the background to the declaration by Jesus: "I am the true vine" (John 15:1). Humanity has failed to produce the fruit of good works. Only Jesus has produced a true harvest of righteousness.

But there is hope for us. We can be fruitful by remaining in Christ. "I am the vine," Jesus says in John 15:5; "you are the branches. If you remain in me and I in you, you will bear much fruit; apart from me you can do nothing."

## Apply

God invites his people to come to him for refuge and to make peace with him (Isaiah 27:5). Jesus invites us to remain in him by listening to his word and obeying him (John 15:3, 7, 10). The result will be fruit that fills all the world (Isaiah 27:6)—"fruit that will last" (John 15:16).

- ❷ *How can you put these things into action today?*
- ❷ *What fruit do you particularly long to see in your life and in the lives of those around you?*
- ❷ *How can you encourage others to take refuge in Christ and remain in him, too?*

# Misplaced confidence

*Where do you place your confidence? In human things? Or in God alone?*

Back in chapters 7 – 8, Isaiah had invited Ahaz, the king of Judah, to trust in God in the face of threats from Aram and Israel. But Ahaz instead formed an alliance with Assyria. For a while that looked like a good option. But now Assyria itself has become the big threat. Judah (now ruled by King Hezekiah) has jumped out of the frying pan and into the mother of all fires.

It's into this situation that Isaiah now speaks in Isaiah 28 – 33.

## The wrong beauty

First of all Isaiah speaks to Israel, the northern kingdom. They were the first to be overrun by the Assyrians.

**Read Isaiah 28:1-13**

❓ *How is Ephraim (another name for Israel) described (v 1, 4)?*

❓ *What will happen to its "wreath"— which represents its pride (v 3)?*

❓ *What is the better wreath Isaiah describes (v 5-6)?*

Ephraim is full of national pride and self-confidence. But their trust is misplaced. Isaiah exposes the futility of human strength and beauty. True beauty, strength and justice are found with God alone.

## The wrong wisdom

In verses 9-10 Isaiah describes the reaction to his ministry. Verse 10 appears to be the equivalent of "Blah, blah, blah". That's what the people say when Isaiah speaks. They prefer the visions of drunken prophets (v 7-8). They don't want to listen to God's word.

So God responds: "Very well then" (v 11). If the people say God's words are "blah, blah, blah," then "blah, blah, blah" is what they will hear: the foreign words of a foreign army. The language spoken on their streets will be Assyrian, and it will be coming from the lips of an invading army.

## ⌃ Pray

Many people today don't want to listen to God's word. This can include Christians. We are so busy that we wonder why we can't hear God's voice or feel his presence. I don't mean hearing words or voices literally, but hearing God speak personally to us through his word.

❓ *Do you ever fall into the trap of drowning out God's voice?*

Pray to him now, asking him to speak through his word today and committing yourself to respond in obedience.

# God's strange work

*It's easy to feel as if God has gone AWOL—absent without leave. We know what we want him to be doing, but he isn't doing it!*

❓ *What would you say God is doing in your life right now? Or does it feel as if he's gone AWOL?*

❓ *How have you seen God work in strange or unexpected ways in the past?*

## Two audiences

So far in Isaiah 28, the prophet has appeared to be speaking to the northern kingdom of Israel. But this sermon is also a message for the southern kingdom of Judah. They should look at what's happened to Israel—who trusted their own strength and wisdom, but ended up being wiped out by Assyria—and learn the lesson.

The reason for the message is that Judah is not learning the lessons of the past. They are seeking the help of another superpower, Egypt, to combat the threat of Assyria—even though an alliance with a superpower is how they got into this problem in the first place!

### Read Isaiah 28:14-22

In verse 15, Isaiah mocks the claims of the people of Judah. They've entered into a covenant with Egypt. More like a covenant with death, says Isaiah. They have made Pharaoh their refuge—but Isaiah says they have made a lie their refuge.

❓ *In verses 17-19, how does Isaiah pick up on each of the claims in verse 15? What does he say will happen?*

## Strange work

Like Israel, Judah will face disaster. Instead of fighting for his people, as God previously did at Mount Perazim and the Valley of Gibeon (see 2 Samuel 5:17-21; Joshua 10:1-11), he will now fight against his people.

God is at work—he has not gone AWOL. But it is not what his people want him to be doing. Isaiah describes it as God's "strange work" (Isaiah 28:21).

## Carefully measured

### Read Isaiah 28:23-29

❓ *How does Isaiah highlight the proportionate, carefully measured work of a farmer in these verses?*

❓ *Some of the farmer's work is violent, but what is his ultimate goal?*

❓ *What does this suggest about God's destructive work?*

## ⌃ Pray

Does it feel as though God is doing "strange work" in your life—or in the life of someone you know? Use this passage to reflect and pray about that situation. Ask God to help you see how he is making you (or your friend) more like Jesus. Praise him that his plans are always "wonderful" and "magnificent" (v 29).

# Victory's secret

*This and the next psalm form a nice little pair. They are royal songs to be sung at the start (Psalm 20) and the conclusion (Psalm 21) of a military campaign.*

## Prayers for the king
### Read Psalm 20:1-3

> ❓ *What is David praying for?*
> ❓ *What do these requests reveal about what he knows about himself and God?*

The temple priests make a genuine plea for God to help their king in the coming battle. But this is no jingoistic song—quite the opposite. It recognises that the battle will be tough—there will be distress (v 1). It acknowledges that he needs God's intervention and help. And it recognises that only those in right relationship with God can appeal for such help (v 3).

## ☑ Apply

Does this psalm sanction the blessing of tanks as they roll out to war? Probably not. Because the real application here is to our struggle as the people of God against the forces of the world, the flesh and the devil. And we need to make the same precautions: to ensure that we're in right standing with the Lord, and that we're depending on him for what will be a bloody, bruising encounter that may regularly leave us in distress.

## Shout for victory
### Read Psalm 20:4-9

> ❓ *Where does victory come from?*
> ❓ *So what is the key to victory?*

The song looks forward to the triumph of God and his anointed king over the enemy. But it is not a foregone conclusion; it is no magic formula for success. Because it still requires:

- plans (v 4)—which God must bless.
- trust (v 7)—in God's power rather than our skill or weaponry.
- God's intervention (v 6)—even with superior numbers and tactics, God's involvement is the only thing that will ensure victory.

···· **TIME OUT** ····································

Israel had plenty of experience of God's way of victory. See 1 Samuel 13:5, 22; 14:1-23.

## ☑ Apply

> ❓ *So what are you trusting in for yourself, or for your church?*
> - *Is it your experience and wisdom as a believer?*
> - *Is it the pulling power of a famous speaker?*
> - *Is it a well-set-up organisation that is effectively administered?*
> - *Is it competent music, social media and livestream capabilities?*

You know, don't you, that they are all worthless without the Lord's blessing...

# A better foundation

*There's one more thing to see in Isaiah 28 about God's strange, destructive work.*

Sometimes it's hard to understand what God is up to. It's not just that it doesn't fit with what we want. It doesn't seem to fit with some of the things the Bible says about God. God is a father, but what kind of father makes his children ill? God is kind, so why does he send hardship into my life? God is love, so why does he allow so many people to take the road to hell? It seems as if God is being unkind and unloving.

But all is not what it seems. God may destroy, but when he is dealing with his people, he destroys only so that he can bring life.

**Read Isaiah 28:15-22**

- ❷ *What does God say he will sweep away in this passage?*
- ❷ *But what does he build in its place (v 16)?*
- ❷ *What is different about this?*

The New Testament says that this cornerstone is Jesus (1 Peter 2:4-8). When everything else comes crashing down, the sure foundation is Jesus. God destroys so that he can build, and Jesus is the foundation and cornerstone of that building. So what do you do when it feels like God has gone AWOL? You look to the cross.

⋯ **TIME OUT** ⋯⋯⋯⋯⋯⋯⋯⋯⋯⋯⋯⋯⋯⋯⋯⋯⋯⋯⋯⋯⋯⋯⋯

**Read 1 Peter 2:4-9**

- ❷ *What is the "house" which God builds on Jesus' foundations (v 5)?*

- ❷ *How do we get to be part of it (v 4)?*
- ❷ *What's our purpose now (v 9)?*

## ⌄ Apply

Isaiah 28 has shown us that human strength, wisdom and beauty will all fail. But God gives us a better place to turn when it feels like everything in which we take refuge is being swept away.

- ❷ *What things do you take refuge in, or hope for?*
- ❷ *How is Christ better than those things?*
- ❷ *In what ways can you start building on his foundation instead of on those human things?*

## The strangest work

The cross is God's ultimate "strange work". It was an act of judgment that brought forgiveness, an act of abandonment that brought reconciliation, and an act of defeat that brought victory.

In the midst of pain and confusion, it may seem as if God doesn't care. But at the cross we see the full extent of God's love. Looking to the cross means we can trust that God is at work for our good, even if he seems to bring only destruction.

## ⌃ Pray

Praise Jesus for the cross and ask for God's help in making him your foundation.

# Warnings and promises

*How do you get someone's attention when they're just not listening?*

Isaiah 28 – 33 contains a series of "sermons", all of which begin with the word "Woe" or, more literally, an attention-grabbing declaration akin to "Hey".

Isaiah is repeatedly warning the people of Judah, whose capital is Jerusalem (called Ariel, for reasons which are unclear, in Isaiah 29).

**Read Isaiah 29:1, 15-16; 30:1-2; 31:1**

- ❓ *Who is Isaiah addressing in these verses?*
- ❓ *What is the problem with what these people are doing?*
- ❓ *What should they be doing instead?*
- ❓ *How do the words used to describe God in 29:16 and 31:1 serve as a motivation to obey him?*

Throughout this section Isaiah is denouncing the blindness and folly of the people. As we've already seen in chapter 28, he calls them to depend on God instead of on human strength and wisdom.

## ⌄ Apply

- ❓ *What difficult situations are you facing now? What about others in your church?*
- ❓ *Look back at the mistakes the people of Judah made. What would it look like for you to make the same mistakes?*
- ❓ *What will it look like to respond with trust in God instead?*
- ❓ *How can you make sure you pay attention to God in these circumstances?*

## Look and see
### Read Isaiah 33:1-24

Once again, Isaiah proclaims the futility of a treaty with Egypt (v 7-14). But he also promises something else.

- ❓ *In verse 7 Isaiah calls the people to "look". What do they see in verses 7-9?*
- ❓ *But who will be "lifted up" (v 10, 15-16)?*
- ❓ *Who will be seen then—and who won't be, anymore (v 17-19)?*
- ❓ *What will the people see when they look at Jerusalem (v 20)?*

Rivers will bring trade to Jerusalem, but no warships will threaten it (v 21). At the moment Jerusalem is like an ill-prepared galleon, but in the future it will enjoy the spoils of victory (v 23). People's sickness will be healed and their sins will be forgiven (v 24).

This vision began to be fulfilled with the first coming of Jesus, and it will be consummated at his second coming.

## ⌃ Pray

In the meantime, Isaiah gives a prayer to pray and a promise to trust.

### Re-read Isaiah 33:2-6

Bring the difficult situations you know of before the Lord. Use the words in Isaiah 33:2-6 to help you pray.

# The desert blooms

*The last two chapters of this section of Isaiah sum up its combination of terrible warnings and wonderful promises.*

Isaiah 34 sees the prophet proclaim God's final judgment on all nations—and then specifically on the nation of Edom.

Edom's territory is so depopulated that it now belongs to wild animals (34:10-15). But in chapter 35, God promises that the desert will bloom again.

**Read Isaiah 35:1-10**

This is a vision of the future—our future, not just Isaiah's. After God judges all the nations (34:1-2), he will renew creation.

> ❷ *How will the desert change (35:1-2, 6-7)?*
> ❷ *What is the source of the splendour it will enjoy (v 2)?*

It's not only the land that will be renewed. God will give sight to the blind and hearing to the deaf (v 5). Previously people have refused to hear God, but now they will see and hear him clearly.

···· TIME OUT ····································

Isaiah already promised this in 32:1-4. Here, it is when the king of righteousness comes that the blind see and fools become wise. The king of righteousness is a reference to Jesus. So this promise was literally fulfilled when Jesus cured those who were blind, and it is metaphorically fulfilled whenever someone becomes a Christian.

## Highway to Zion

Isaiah 35:8-10 describes how God will gather his people home.

> ❷ *Who will get to walk on God's new "highway" (v 8-10)?*
> ❷ *What will they do when they reach their destination?*

We have a preview of this future in the ministry of Jesus (see, for example, Luke 7:21-22). But this promise will ultimately be fulfilled in the renewal of all things when Jesus returns in glory.

## ▲ Pray

"Only the redeemed will walk there, and those the LORD has rescued will return" (Isaiah 35:9-10).

> ❷ *Who would you like to see rescued and redeemed by God? Pray for them now.*

In Isaiah 28 – 35 we have read a lot of warnings and promises. Spend some time reflecting on these and asking for God's help in living the kind of faith to which Isaiah has been calling us.

# The army at the gates

*In Isaiah 36 – 39, we turn from prophetic oracle to historical narrative.*

The Assyrian army has invaded Judah and has arrived at the gates of Jerusalem. Egypt, which had promised to help, is nowhere to be seen. In Isaiah 36, Sennacherib (the king of Assyria) sends his field commander to meet a delegation of officials from Judah's King Hezekiah.

The location of this meeting at the Upper Pool (v 2) is significant. This is where Isaiah met King Ahaz (Hezekiah's father) in 7:3. Back then God offered to rescue Ahaz from the threat posed by Aram and the northern tribes of Israel, but Ahaz chose to look for help from Assyria instead. Now Assyria has become the threat, and Hezekiah faces a similar dilemma: trust in God, or seek help from elsewhere?

**Read Isaiah 36:13-20**

- *What reason does the commander give not to trust God?*
- *Who does he say the people should trust instead, and why?*

The theology of Assyria is clear. No god can stand against the power of the Assyrian military machine. The commander's claim is that Sennacherib is more powerful than the LORD, and his word is more trustworthy.

## The key issue

**Read Isaiah 37:1-7**

- *How does Hezekiah feel about what's going on (v 3)?*
- *What does he hope that God will do?*

Hezekiah sees clearly that the issue is the LORD's reputation. In the following verses, Isaiah agrees: "This is what the LORD says ... the underlings of the king of Assyria have blasphemed me" (v 6).

The claims of the Assyrians are powerful. But Hezekiah and Isaiah know that they are lies. They will have confidence in God instead.

- *What does Isaiah promise will happen (v 7)?*
- *How do you think Hezekiah felt at that point?*

## Apply

- *Have you ever faced ridicule or attack for your faith like the people of Jerusalem did? What did your attacker say about God?*
- *How did you respond? Did you think that God's reputation was a key issue?*
- *Why do you think God's reputation is so important to him?*
- *What do you think it would look like to respond to attackers in a way that upholds God's reputation first and foremost?*
- *In what other ways might we show people that we have confidence in God?*

# Hezekiah's prayer

*"Do not let the god you depend on deceive you," the Assyrian king tells Hezekiah (Isaiah 37:10). But Hezekiah knows the truth—and he sticks to it.*

**Read Isaiah 37:9-20**

❓ *How does Sennacherib attack God's reputation once again in his message to Hezekiah?*

❓ *What do you think you would do if you were in Hezekiah's shoes?*

❓ *What does he do, first of all (v 14)?*

## Enacted prayer

It's not that Hezekiah is providing God with information of which God is unaware. It's a kind of enacted prayer: a deliberate act through which Hezekiah brings his problem tangibly before God. It's a practice you might find helpful from time to time. Find some physical embodiment of your problem and "spread it out before the LORD".

## Confident prayer

The way Hezekiah begins his prayer might seem to us like "filler": stock phrases to pad out prayer, or a warm-up before we get to the important content of our requests. But remember the situation that Hezekiah is facing. Sennacherib has claimed that God is untrustworthy and powerless. Hezekiah is declaring that this is a lie.

❓ *How do each of the phrases in verse 16 function as a response to what Sennacherib has said?*

❓ *How do these phrases give Hezekiah confidence?*

Hezekiah's description of God as "enthroned between the cherubim" (v 16) is more than just a claim that God is encircled by angels. This is referring to the ark in the temple, which had two cherubim on top. Between them was the atonement cover (Exodus 35:12)—the place where atonement was made by the high priest on the Day of Atonement (Leviticus 16:15-16). So this is a pointer to the fact that God shows mercy.

❓ *There are more phrases describing God in Isaiah 37:17, 20. What does Hezekiah ask on the basis of what he knows God is like?*

## Big-picture prayer

The final phrases of Hezekiah's prayer reveal that it is not only a request for deliverance but a request for God to magnify his name. His prayer reflects his concern for God's glory. Jesus, too, taught us to begin by asking God to honour his name ("Hallowed be your name", Luke 11:2).

## ⌃ Pray

What fearful or difficult situations do you or others you know face at the moment? Take some time to reflect on the descriptions of God that Hezekiah gives in these verses. Then write a prayer of your own, in which your requests are based on who God is and how he might be glorified.

# God's answer

*Hezekiah has prayed in faith. He doesn't have to wait long to hear God's reply.*

## The tables turn

**Read Isaiah 37:21-29**

Isaiah promises that the Assyrians will not enter Jerusalem—which is why she's called a "Virgin" in verse 22. Instead, Sennacherib will go home in disgrace.

- ❓ *Who did Sennacherib mock (v 23-24)?*
- ❓ *Who is being mocked now (v 22)?*
- ❓ *What did Sennacherib boast about (v 24-25)?*
- ❓ *But how does God reinterpret what Sennacherib has done (v 26)?*
- ❓ *How else will the tables turn (v 28-29)?*

## National renewal

**Read Isaiah 37:30-32**

The second part of God's response is addressed to Hezekiah.

- ❓ *What does God promise about the economy?*
- ❓ *What does he promise about the people?*
- ❓ *How can Hezekiah be sure that this will happen?*

## A promise kept

**Read Isaiah 37:33-35**

- ❓ *What promises does God make here?*

The second oracle ends, "The zeal of the LORD Almighty will accomplish this" (v 32), while the third ends, "I will defend this city and save it, for my sake and for the sake of David my servant!" (v 35) God is zealous. He is passionate about his glory. And so he will save Jerusalem "for my sake"—that is, to vindicate the honour of his reputation. He will also save Jerusalem "for the sake of David my servant"—that is, to fulfil his promise that one of David's sons would always reign over God's people (2 Samuel 7:15-16).

**Read Isaiah 37:36-38**

What God promised duly happened. The remarkable thing about this account of Jerusalem's deliverance is how brief it is! The writer took a long time to set the scene of Assyrian provocation, and we want him to balance this out with an extended description of Sennacherib's comeuppance. Perhaps the point is to stress Hezekiah's faith. Despite lots of reasons to submit to Assyria, he trusts God—and this leads to God's glory. All the kingdoms of the earth do learn that the LORD is the only God. It's a prayer that is still being answered as we read these words!

## ⌃ Pray

Praise God for all the times he has defended and saved you—ultimately through Jesus on the cross, but also in any smaller-scale ways you can think of. Ask that his name might be glorified in all the earth.

# Where honour is due

*This victory psalm, presumably to be sung after a successful campaign, falls neatly into two halves.*

## A song for the king
### Read Psalm 21:1-7

> ❓ *What trap do victorious armies and generals fall into?*
> ❓ *How is a different attitude expressed here?*

The first section is sung to God by the worship leader and praises God for answering the prayers of Psalm 20. How slow we are to do that for ourselves; to give praise to God when "it all works out as we had hoped". Perhaps keeping a record of our prayer requests would help us to persevere at asking, and be more faithful at being thankful for the answers.

Notice that all the honour and glory goes to God. "You have granted him his heart's desire" (21:2); "You came to greet him with rich blessings..." (v 3); "He asked you for life, and you gave it to him..." (v 4); " you have bestowed on him splendour and majesty" (v 5). There is no room for boasting or pride here. Even the highest of the high owes *everything* to God.

## ⌄ Apply

It's an almost universal response. When something goes wrong, lay the blame at someone else's feet. But when it goes right, then pull as much glory to yourself as you can. They're both responses that believers will be battling with. Are you?

> ❓ *How does 1 John 1:10 and 2:15-17 help?*

## A song of victory
### Read Psalm 21:8-13

The singer now turns to the king and describes the thoroughness with which he will deal with the enemy. Their plots will fail. They will be blotted out and consumed in a blazing inferno. Such was and is the fate of all who set themselves against the one true God.

Passages such as this have been wrongly applied to nations, promoting the "God is on our side" mentality. We're on much safer ground applying it to the confidence we can have in God's kingdom winning through against the powers of darkness.

## ⌄ Apply

At a deeper level, this psalm is also about the victory that the Lord Jesus has won, about God raising him from the grave to live "for ever and ever..." (v 4).

Read the psalm again, and rejoice with the writer in God's overwhelming victory for his anointed King, Jesus, and for the ultimate defeat of all evil.

## ⌃ Pray
### Read Luke 17:11-19

Talk to the Lord about your response.

# Fresh deliverance

*The Assyrians have gone and deliverance has come. But the drama isn't over for Hezekiah.*

The king becomes extremely ill and is at the point of death.

**Read Isaiah 38:1-8**

> ❓ *What does Isaiah advise Hezekiah to do (v 1)?*
> ❓ *On what basis does Hezekiah ask God for deliverance (v 3)?*
> ❓ *How does God respond?*

## A song of deliverance

**Read Isaiah 38:9-22**

Hezekiah begins his song of response with a powerful series of images depicting human frailty (v 10-14).

> ❓ *How do Hezekiah's emotions come across here?*
> ❓ *What's his relationship with the Lord in verse 11, verses 12-13, and verse 14?*
> ❓ *How will he respond now that he's recovered (v 15)?*

## Reasons for recovery

> ❓ *Why does Hezekiah think that God allowed this suffering (v 17)?*
> ❓ *In what sense might Hezekiah's illness have benefited him?*

"The wages of sin is death," says Paul in Romans 6:23. But Hezekiah receives life instead of death because God has overlooked his sins. This was a temporary measure, but it points to the ultimate and enduring solution for sin, when Christ would pay the penalty for sin on the cross. This would lead not just to 15 extra years of life for Hezekiah but eternal life for all who belong to him.

> ❓ *Why else does Hezekiah think God saved him (v 18-19)? (Hint: What can Hezekiah only do if he's alive?)*

Again, for Hezekiah this was only temporary. But when those who are in Christ are raised to eternal life, we will praise God for ever.

## ⌄ Apply

> ❓ *How would you sum up how Hezekiah makes sense of his suffering and recovery?*
> ❓ *What would it look like for us to make sense of our own sorrows and joys in a similar way?*
> ❓ *How does Hezekiah say he will respond to what has happened (v 15, 19, 20)?*
> ❓ *Again, what would it look like for us to respond this way, both in good times and in bad?*

## ⌃ Pray

Spend some time reflecting on Hezekiah's song. Try reading it aloud a few times. Then respond in prayer and praise.

*Bible in a year: Exodus 14-15 • 1 Thessalonians 3*

# A poignant postscript

*Hezekiah has seen off the world's superpower, and he has come back from the brink of death.*

At this point those following Isaiah's ministry might be wondering whether Hezekiah is the shoot promised from the stump of Jesse (Isaiah 11:1)—a descendant of David who would rule over the nations.

But this story ends in tragedy.

## Ominous visitors

**Read Isaiah 39:1-8**

It seems that Hezekiah's success has gone to his head. In his pride he shows the Babylonian envoys all his splendours. It may have been part of negotiating a pact with Babylon—the kind of pact that his father had disastrously made with Assyria and that he himself may have made with Egypt. (Marduk-Baladan led a decade-long revolt against Assyria and may have wanted Hezekiah's support.)

> ❷ What do you think is the tone of Isaiah's question in verse 3?

Isaiah's prediction in verses 5-7 picks up Hezekiah's "everything" language.

> ❷ What will happen to everything Hezekiah showed the Babylonians?

This forms a poignant postscript to Hezekiah's story. "Hezekiah trusted in the Lord, the God of Israel," says 2 Kings 18:5. "There was no one like him among all the kings of Judah, either before him or after him." It is the highest possible praise. Yet Hezekiah was not the messianic king who would

restore God's reign over the earth. Instead, his story ends with a sense of foreboding. It prepares us for the remainder of the book of Isaiah, in which Isaiah addresses those caught up in the exile that Hezekiah has precipitated.

After reading Isaiah 36 – 37, we might ask, "Why did Judah end up in exile when God could respond to their faith with such remarkable acts of deliverance?" What chapters 38 – 39 remind us of is that the faith shown in chapters 36 – 37 was the exception rather than the norm. The scene is set for Isaiah's prophecy of the Servant of God, who will end the exile and restore God's reign. That comes in chapter 40.

## Good?

> ❷ Why does Hezekiah say that what Isaiah has prophesied is good (39:8)?
> ❷ How does this contrast with Hezekiah's previous priorities (see 37:20; 38:3, 17-20)?

## ⌃ Pray

Your faith and mine is often just as flaky and inconsistent as Hezekiah's. Thankfully, we have Jesus, the "pioneer and perfecter of faith" (Hebrews 12:2). It is through him and by him that we can come to God.

Spend some time praising God for the faith he has given us, and committing yourself to Jesus afresh.

# LUKE: Prepare the way

*The second act of Luke's story starts with a form that must have seemed familiar to both a Roman audience, and a Jewish readership who knew their Old Testaments.*

## A prophet
### Read Luke 3:1-6

- ❷ *What would a pagan Roman audience make of the first two verses?*
- ❷ *What would these same verses bring to mind for a Jewish audience (see Haggai 1:1 and Isaiah 1:1 for example)?*

This is a historical account. But it is so much more. By echoing the language of many prophetic OT books, Luke immediately raises our eyes to the point he is making here in Luke 3:1-6: John is a prophet who comes with a purpose from God.

- ❷ *What is that purpose and what is his message?*
- ❷ *Why must people repent?*
- ❷ *How do people show that they have responded to that message?*
- ❷ *What will happen as people repent?*
- ❷ *How is this a departure from the Old Testament way of thinking about sin?*

John is filled with glorious purpose. The Lord is coming, and in order to prepare for this momentous event, there is an urgent need to get ready. People must turn away from their sins and show they are serious by undergoing a public baptism. Only then will they receive forgiveness.

**···· TIME OUT** ··········································

What is at issue here is the question of whether someone is a true Israelite or not. The sacrificial system has not been bypassed or nullified, but there is a prior question: are you truly a member of the people of God? Historians speculate as to the local situation in Jordan and Galilee—a region where Greek and Roman influence had been growing. Near Nazareth a new Greek-speaking town called Sepphoris was growing rapidly. Perhaps Joseph the builder and his son spent time there building houses. John calls people to be true to their calling as God's people in preparation for the day of the Lord.

## A promise
### Re-read Luke 3:4-6

- ❷ *What are the big promises here?*
- ❷ *How might this impact Luke's first readers?*

The coming of the Lord to Israel was never about simply reinstating Israel as God's people in God's place under God's chosen king. It marked a step change in God's purposes in the world. What was once the privilege of a few will become the invitation to the many. The events that will unfold will bring salvation to the ends of the earth.

## ☑ Apply

- ❷ *That message is still spreading. What might you need to repent of to enable straight paths to be made for the Lord to come to your friends, family and neighbours?*

# Firebrand

*We tend to look down a little on firebrand preachers these days. And yet John had a knack for "saying it like it is". Perhaps we need more preachers like him today...*

## Vipers

**Read Luke 3:7-9**

- ❓ *What are the indications that John's message is popular here?*
- ❓ *So why would he preach to them in this way? What does he know about the human heart?*
- ❓ *What are his essential messages in these verses?*

John is wildly successful. Moved by his message, crowds are flocking to him to be baptised so that their sins could be forgiven. And yet he greets them with insults. We might not use John to train our greeters at the church door, but he understands what is truly going on. People may be moved by a message, but the response can so often be mere religiosity. *I'll go through the ritual—everyone else is.* But the matter of real change is a very different thing. The water changes nothing. Forgiveness only comes when repentance is real, and that is shown by a change in our thinking and living in everyday life.

## ⌃ Pray

It is the same today. We can be committed church members and love the singing, the fellowship, the Bible studies, the preaching. But is there evidence that our lives have changed—that repentance is real? Talk to the Lord about yourself and your church.

## Practical religion

**Read Luke 3:10-14**

- ❓ *What is the surprising answer to the question in verse 10?*
- ❓ *What are the signs of genuine repentance for tax collectors and soldiers?*

Honesty, integrity, compassion, generosity, humility, contentment. These are all things we admire in others, and yet so often religion can be a cloak for the opposite as many recent scandals have shown. John understood the depth and reality of our sinful hearts. We are quick to manipulate and use the good gifts God has given us to indulge our dishonesty, hypocrisy, indifference, meanness, pride and lust for more. A venomous viper lurks within us. No wonder God's wrath is kindled against us.

## ⌄ Apply

Luke gives us little vignettes of John's message to soldiers, tax collectors and the crowd. What do you think he might say to you wherever you are: student, mother, retiree, office worker?

John's call to acts of compassion can feel a little awkward to us now. Are we sometimes a little afraid of preaching the need for practical compassion, as though this somehow compromises the gospel?

- ❓ *Is this kind of compassion part of your discipleship response?*

# The real baptism

*Powerful preachers attract strong followings. And then the danger is that they are exalted and put on a pedestal. John is aware of this danger and rejects it.*

## Who are you?
### Read Luke 3:15-18

❷ *How does John answer the unspoken question of verse 15?*
❷ *How is John different to the Messiah?*
❷ *How does John reinforce his message to them?*

"More powerful than I." *Wow!* John's sermons were raging tornadoes—so what would the one to come be like? John just made people wet as they promised to change their ways in the face of God's impending arrival. But the Messiah would do something deeper, stronger, more powerful as he would pour the Holy Spirit into people's lives, and refine them with fire. Notice that John didn't just issue this as a statement, denying the rumour that he was the Messiah. He repeated it again and again (v 18). As scary as it might seem, this would be good news for people.

## ☑ Apply

Jesus will gather, sift and separate. He will judge and destroy those who are fake followers. But he will transform those who genuinely turn to him as he pours the life and power of God into their lives. And this is good news. John's message is the same as our message today.

❷ *Are you clear about that?*

## Truth to power
### Read Luke 3:19-20

❷ *Why does John get involved in politics?*
❷ *What results from this?*
❷ *What effect might his imprisonment have had on the crowd?*

One of the roles of the Old Testament prophets was to "speak truth to power". And we might feel a little uncomfortable about this. Is it really the job of the church to get involved in these things? Shouldn't we just keep quiet and get on with the job of sharing the gospel with others; shouldn't we keep politics out of the pulpit?

Party politics certainly. But issues of social justice never. We may differ on how problems are to be best solved, but Christians should always be in the forefront of fighting injustice, poverty and calling out evil as we see it. Wilberforce, Shaftesbury, Fry, Bonhoeffer and many others picked up this struggle at immense cost to themselves.

## ☑ Apply

❷ *Are you, and is your church, involved in "practical religion" of this kind?*
❷ *What can you do to change this today?*
❷ *Are you prepared for what it might cost?*

# Credentials

*And now John's cousin reappears on the stage. He is just another figure in the crowds that swarmed around John, and yet John's removal marks the start of his ministry.*

## Qualified by God
### Read Luke 3:21-22

- ❓ *Why was Jesus baptised when he neither needed repentance, nor the forgiveness of sins?*
- ❓ *What Old Testament echoes are there in the description in verse 22?*
- ❓ *What does the voice from heaven say, and why is this important?*

The scene brings to mind Genesis 1:1 where the Spirit of God hovers like a bird over the face of the water—just before God's word brings order and sense to a chaotic formless void. The implications are powerful. This is a profound and significant moment, signalling that what happens next is of equal and perhaps even greater significance. God's powerful, creative word is about to be spoken.

Just as baptism marked a new start for God's repentant people; Jesus' baptism marks a new chapter in his life. His ministry begins. But we are left wondering, *who is this man?* John suggested he would come with fire and almost violent action. And yet the voice from heaven declares love, pleasure and satisfaction with the Son. So what will his ministry be like? We must wait and see.

## Qualified by heritage
### Read Luke 3:23-38

- ❓ *What names jump out at you from this list?*
- ❓ *What theological points are being made?*
- ❓ *How does this list show Jesus' qualifications for his roles as prophet, priest and king?*

There is a continuing fascination today with genealogies—peering into the lives of our past ancestors to discover wealth, fame, intrigue or notoriety. Some dark family secrets have also come to light as I have examined my ancestry. But this is not a list designed to demonstrate some legal entitlement to land or wealth. It is here to show how the Lord Jesus is the culmination of God's promises. He is descended from Israel's last true king, Zerubbabel (v 27, see Haggai 2:23); he is a descendent of David, to whom God promised a throne for ever; he is a son of Abraham to whom God made great promises of blessing for the world; and of course a son of Adam who was promised that one of his descendents would crush the serpent's head, and remove the curse for ever. The stage is set for the momentous events that follow.

## 🔼 Pray

If you are in Christ, you can hear and own the same words as the Lord Jesus heard on that day: "You are my Son whom I love; with you I am well pleased". Rejoice in that now as you talk to your heavenly Father.

# Man of sorrows

*Psalms often have a "double horizon". They look to immediate events, but also look forward to a greater fulfilment. This is no clearer than in today's psalm.*

## David's sorrow

**Read Psalm 22:1-11**

> ❓ *What is David's situation?*
> ❓ *What makes it even more distressing?*

Suffering of any sort is hard. But there are some things which make it harder to bear. On David's immediate horizon, he is writing about his own suffering—he feels abandoned by God. He's in dire trouble (v 1), from which there seems no escape. He cries out in prayer, but heaven seems to maintain a stony silence (v 2).

> ❓ *Have you ever felt like this?*

## Jesus' sorrow

**Read Mark 15:21-34**

On the further horizon, as David writes about his own situation, he is also writing about King Jesus who would come to die to end all suffering. God-forsakenness is at the heart of the cross. It is the great cosmic swap, where our sins were exchanged for Christ's righteousness; where the Son of God experienced the forsakenness that our sins deserve. This psalm gives us an insight into the horrifying reality of the cross.

Read the verses from Psalm 22 again and spend some time pondering each of the points below...

- Abandoned for you (Psalm 22:1-2): we can think of Jesus' separation from his Father as a theological idea, and forget what it was actually like.

- Trusting for you (v 3-5): we can imagine too, that death was not a big thing for the Lord; after all, he was going to be raised again. But think again. He faced death with the same resources we have: trust in God's promises and his track record of saving those he loves.

- Mocked for you (v 6-8): he could have called 10,000 angels at any moment to wipe out the cruel scoffers and the vindictive anger of the crowd. But he didn't... there was something more important on his mind—*you and me.*

- Living for you (v 9-10): since before his birth, this is the road he trod, trusting his Father at every point along the way.

- Alone for you (v 11): even his closest friends had deserted him—the very people he was suffering for.

## ⌃ Pray

Amazing grace! The Lord of the universe, your Creator and master, endured and suffered all these things—for you!

Work through the list again, and humbly thank your Lord and God.

# Qualified by testing

*We've already seen how Jesus is qualified by his ancestry and by the direct endorsement of his Father. But there is another way he must show his qualification.*

## The desert

**Read Luke 4:1-2**

❷ *Whose idea was this testing (v 1)?*
❷ *What is the significance of the place and the duration of this test? What Old Testament story does it bring to mind?*

In the Old Testament, God uses the name "son" for both his people, Israel, and their king as their leader and representative. And here we see the Son of God pass through water and enter the desert for 40 days. The symbolism is clear. The Lord Jesus is undergoing the same test as the people of Israel did after passing through the waters of the Red Sea. They failed the test miserably. Although only 40 days, the Son's test is more rigorous. Israel had been given manna and quails to live off. Jesus ate nothing. This experience would lead anyone to be at their most vulnerable. Notice that these temptations were constant during that time. This test is no game; it is severe and rigorous.

## The tests

**Read Luke 4:3-13**

❷ *What can we learn from the nature of the three temptations?*
❷ *What can we learn about Jesus' defence, and what it shows about him?*
❷ *Which do you think is the odd one out?*

Some have noted that all three temptations are alternatives to gaining a following, but without the cross. If you feed people, or dazzle them with miracles, or take hold of supreme authority, people will follow you, but the world remains the same. People are still lost in their sins, and, ultimately, under the dominion of darkness. This is not what Jesus came to do. To embrace any of these offers would be to become a false messiah—a wolf, not the Good Shepherd.

Intriguingly, the Lord did provide bread, and perform astonishing miracles. But he did this for others, not himself, and always out of compassion, not self-promotion. But while many accused him of being a devil-worshipper, he never bowed the knee before the tempter—even when severely tempted in Gethsemane.

## ✓ Apply

Temptation can be resisted. But we need the help from above to do it. Jesus' persistent resistance under sustained pressure should be inspiring for us, as is the promise in 1 Corinthians 10:11-13. But even when we fail, we know that we can find forgiveness because he did not fail.

❷ *How does this comfort and challenge you today?*

## ⌃ Pray

Give thanks to God for Jesus. This severe test was just the start of three more years of struggle—and he did it for you.

# Mission statement

*And so it starts. This man, this ministry, this mission—it has all been planned since the dawn of time, and the last 30 years have been a preparation for all that follows.*

## Popular preacher

**Read Luke 4:14-15**

- ❓ *What does Jesus do and what is the response?*
- ❓ *What is his inspiration and strength for this?*

## Provocative message

**Read Luke 4:16-22**

- ❓ *Why is the passage Jesus chose to read so provocative?*
- ❓ *How is his statement even more provocative?*
- ❓ *What is the initial reaction to his sermon?*

Isaiah's prophesy describes a new age of God's rule, when the suffering servant would lead God's people out of shame and oppression to freedom once more. Three times the passage says "me". And Jesus claims that this prophesy applies to him. Perhaps the crowd didn't at first make the connection, so excited were they at the suggestion that they were entering this new age soon. But it becomes pretty clear in what happens next.

## Powerful pushback

**Read Luke 4:23-30**

- ❓ *What background murmurings had Jesus picked up, do you think?*

- ❓ *What is the challenge of verses 24-26 for the people of his home town?*
- ❓ *Why is their response so savage?*

He was clearly already known as a healer and miracle worker, but they could not seem to accept that this son of a local builder was anything special. And when he quotes Scripture and culture to them to reveal their hypocrisy, it's too much for them to bear, and the service turns nasty.

## ☑ Apply

Witnessing to family is always the hardest thing to do. Their familiarity with us makes it especially hard for them to accept the good news we want to share with them. We mean it in love and humility, but it is so easily and conveniently taken as arrogance. We must keep following Jesus' example of being gracious in the way we speak (v 20); and yet firm and clear on what we believe to be the truth about the good news.

## ⌃ Pray

Talk to the Lord about members of your family. Perhaps they have been hostile in the past and you have given up praying for them or trying to get through to them.

Pray for an opportunity this week to speak about the one who gives sight, frees us from oppression and is good news to the poor.

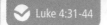

# Proof of identity

*It's one thing to make bold claims about yourself; it's another to prove it. And the greater the claim, the more compelling the evidence must be to back it up.*

## Sermons

**Read Luke 4:31-32**

❓ *What was striking about Jesus' teaching?*
❓ *How did it compare to what they were used to hearing?*

It seems they were used to hearing erudite, reflective, analytical but inconclusive expositions. Jesus' words were a breath of fresh air in the stale atmosphere of the synagogues in Galilee. His words had authority, because *he* had authority. Jesus is Lord of theology.

## ✔ Apply

We too can speak with authority, when it is Jesus' words that we are speaking. When we declare the promises of God and the call to repent and believe, we can speak with a quiet confidence that God himself is issuing his call through us, saying: *be reconciled to God* (see 2 Corinthians 5:20).

## Spirits

**Read Luke 4:33-37**

❓ *What is shocking about this incident?*
❓ *What does the demon know that the onlookers are only dimly aware of?*
❓ *Why does Jesus say "be quiet"?*

The Lord had already faced down Satan himself in the wilderness, but his minions are all around. They know the truth about what he came to do, and are not fearful to speak it, because they know their days are numbered. But the Lord doesn't want them to set the agenda. And this is no showboating for the onlookers. He is simply fulfilling the prophesy from Isaiah that he read earlier. He is freeing someone who is oppressed, out of love and compassion for them.

## Sickness

**Read Luke 4:38-44**

❓ *How is the healing of Simon's mother-in-law a picture of discipleship for us?*
❓ *What does Jesus do after this enormously succesful healing rally (v 42)?*
❓ *What results, and what does this show us about Jesus' priorities?*

Jesus came to be a preacher. The exorcisms, the healings and other miracles authenticated his authority, but were incidental to his mission, which was to reveal the character and purposes of God, and then to go on to fulfil them in his death and resurrection.

## ✔ Apply

Are you easily distracted? There is something to be said for having a clear and simple focus in our life's ministry and work. Many distractions will come our way. Most of them are useful and profitable, but...

❓ *Is there something you need to say "no" to in order to give yourself more freely to something bigger?*

Talk to the Lord about your thoughts.

*Bible in a year: Exodus 34-35 • James 3*

# Gathering the flock

*Jesus already knew Simon Peter well, and had stayed at his home. But now their friendship must move to a new level.*

## Crowds
### Read Luke 5:1-3

- ❓ *What are the signs that Jesus is becoming more popular?*
- ❓ *What is it that draws them to him?*
- ❓ *What is clever about his solution to the problem?*

The Lord has already shown his commitment to preaching above miracles and healings, but the crowds are pressing all around. Teaching from a boat allows him to speak unhindered to a larger crowd without distraction. It has been observed that the water would act as a sound reflector, making his voice more easily heard by more people.

## ✅ Apply

We mustn't be frightened of innovation in the way we reach, teach and present God's word to people. True, there are disadvantages to livestream and Zoom, which can never replace the experience and reality of meeting together in person, but the important thing is that souls hungry to hear the word of God continue to be fed.

- ❓ *What innovations in sharing God's word with others are you reluctant to embrace? Do you have genuine reasons for that, or is it simply your tradition?*

## Fish
### Read Luke 5:4-11

Many of Jesus' miracles are "signs" or enacted parables of some deep spiritual truth he wants to impress upon us.

- ❓ *What is Simon's reaction to Jesus' command? Why?*
- ❓ *What is surprising about Simon's response to this miracle?*
- ❓ *Why does Jesus tell them to "not be afraid" do you think?*

Are we in danger of doing the same thing as Simon? We think we know how the world, church, life, money works; and so we discount a direct command of God because "we know better". Simon realises his arrogance in thinking he knew more than Jesus about fishing; and he sees his sinfulness, as Jesus gives this sign as confirmation that he is the Messiah. Simon feels overwhelmed and unworthy. But Jesus has other ideas. Simon's unworthiness is the reason Jesus came. And now that Simon has glimpsed the big picture of his condition and Jesus' identity, he can be enlisted in the task.

## 🔼 Pray

Talk to the Lord about your unworthiness.

Thank Jesus that he has called you to be a "people-fisher", and ask for the tools, the wisdom and the opportunity to cast a net today.

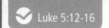
# Making clean

*Simon had seen with startling clarity his own sin and need for forgiveness. But how can we be cleansed from sin? That's the question the rest of the chapter wrestles with.*

## Leprosy

**Read Luke 5:12-14**

- ❓ *What is remarkable about the man's request in verse 12?*
- ❓ *What is even more remarkable about what Jesus does for him?*
- ❓ *What does Jesus say he must now do? Why?*

Skin diseases, and leprosy in particular, were common in the ancient world, even as they are in the wider world today, in places where there is poor access to modern medicine. Those who were afflicted by this disease were put into isolation—cut off from their family, friends, society at large. This is something we understand a little more about after the last two years of COVID lockdowns. But leprosy was also seen as a sign of spiritual separation. Because you could not mingle with God's people and come into the Lord's presence in the temple, you were, quite literally, cut off from God.

And so Jesus' startling, instant, utterly complete healing restores so much more than the leper's skin. He restores him socially and spiritually too. He has come to fulfil the law, not abolish it. He will fulfil the rites of purification through his death on the cross, but for now, the letter of the ritual law must be obeyed. And along the way, he is bearing testimony to the priests and religious authorities that he is the Messiah, and that they do not need to oppose him.

## ☑ Apply

Religious people are looking for all the right things—forgiveness, cleansing, community, truth. They are just looking in the wrong place for it. And the most hostile opposition to the gospel message will always come from religion. This begins to unfold in the next story we read in Luke 5.

- ❓ *How have you experienced that yourself in the past?*
- ❓ *What "testimony" could you give to a religious person that shows them the real way to find cleansing?*

## ⌃ Pray

What is troubling you most at the moment? Talk to the Lord about it, echoing the man's prayer: *"Lord, if you are willing, you can..."*

Leprosy and other medical issues continue to plague millions worldwide. Pray for medical missionaries who continue to bring healing, hope and good news to those who are sick around the world.

## Popularity

**Read Luke 5:15-16**

As Jesus' popularity grows, the demands on him grow too. And so he *must* find the time to maintain and nurture his connection to the source of his strength and resolve.

And so must we.

# Opposition

*His popularity grows and grows, but Jesus is about to become unpopular with one important segment of the crowds that flocked to hear him.*

## Through the roof
### Read Luke 5:17-21

- ❓ *What further signs are there of Jesus' growing popularity?*
- ❓ *How did Jesus "see" their faith (v 20)?*
- ❓ *Why is what Jesus says both shocking and provocative?*

The Lord could see their faith by their determination to get to him. *Nothing* would stop them from bringing their friend to the one person they knew could heal him. But his next words show what the real problem was. Quadriplegia is a terrible thing. But unforgiven sin is far, far worse. And so he speaks first to the biggest problem in the room. But the Pharisees also go through the roof! They are right: only God can forgive sin. The irony in this tense situation is palpable.

## ⌃ Pray

When we "share for prayer" at our Bible studies, the requests often default to illness. One friend calls it "the organ recital": my liver has problems; my auntie's kidneys are failing; my friend has bad lungs, etc. As important as these things are, should we not be much more concerned to cry out to the Lord for our unforgiven friends and family—and stop at nothing to bring them before the only remedy for their deeper soul sickness?

- ❓ *Why not do that now?*

## Mat for sale
### Read Luke 5:22-26

- ❓ *What sign does Jesus give to them of his identity (see v 21-22)?*
- ❓ *What is the surprising answer to the question in verse 23?*
- ❓ *How is this much more than just a healing?*
- ❓ *How does the crowd respond?*

It is, of course, *much* more difficult to forgive sins—but it is also unseen. So in a sense, the astonishing healing—instant, complete and with a single command—can never *prove* that Jesus can forgive sins. But on the other hand, the logical step is not hard to make. If someone can do something as amazing as this, then it doesn't seem like a big step to believe he can also forgive sins—because only God could heal like that. Clearly the crowd understood this as they sat open-mouthed at what had just happened right in front of them. Although they seem content with the spectacle alone: *"We've seen remarkable things today"*.

## ⌄ Apply

- ❓ *As a "people-fisher", what might you say differently to each of the following?*
  - *The paralysed man with a mat for sale*
  - *His friends*
  - *The Pharisees and teachers of the law*
  - *The crowd*

# Dark times

*More miraculous insights into the death of the Lord Jesus from the pen of David.*

## The miracle
**Read Psalm 22:12-21**

> ❓ *What is remarkable about this description, written around 1,000 BC?*

The description of suffering here is extraordinarily accurate for crucifixion, and Jesus' death in particular. The dislocation of the bones (v 14); the terrible thirst (v 15); the piercing of hands and feet (v 16); stripped naked for all to see (v 17); and the casting of lots for his clothes (v 18). And remarkable that, inspired by the Holy Spirit, David writes so powerfully about something he does not know fully.

## The mess

His suffering is both intensely physical, and also emotional...

> ❓ *Track through the verses one by one, and think for a moment about the inward suffering Jesus went through.*

## The mockers

> ❓ *David describes himself as "a worm" (v 6). How does he describe his oppressors?*

The language of this passage describes those who persecute and torture him as animals—bulls, lions, dogs, wild oxen. All the more amazing then to see what Jesus prayed for them...

**Read Luke 23:34**

## ✓ Apply

Many believers experience times, sometimes lasting years, when they feel God has deserted them—illness, or the nagging pain of broken or marred relationships. We should never be glib about the reality of the pain that people experience. But one hard truth that the cross of Christ teaches us is that suffering, in God's mercy, can be both creative and purposeful—even when it doesn't appear so. In fact, as the cross and resurrection show, it's at times when God seems absent that he may be at work in profound and amazing ways.

> ❓ *How can difficulties actually help us grow as his followers?*

**Read 1 Peter 4:12-19** for some answers.

## ⌃ Pray

Pray today for people you know who are going through dark times. Ask our loving Father to help them see that pain can be purposeful. And pray that you would have both the opportunity, and the right words, to encourage them, and give them Christian, cross-centred hope and encouragement.

# Doctor in the house

*I hope you are beginning to see how these simple, straightforward stories are packed with depth, meaning and challenge.*

## Curious choices
**Read Luke 5:27-28**

- ❓ *What do you know about tax collectors in the time of Jesus?*
- ❓ *Why might this make Levi a confusing and provocative choice as a disciple to the onlookers?*
- ❓ *How is Levi's response narrated, and what clues might this give us to what Luke is trying to impress upon us?*

The incidents we have read all point to the amazing authority of Jesus. He says it: it happens. At a word, demons flee, sickness vanishes, useless and withered arms and legs suddenly spring to life, and fish throw themselves into nets. And his word of command to Levi is immediately obeyed. No clarifying questions, no negotiation, just a simple response. His "stuff", money and business were of no interest to him when he heard this voice of command.

## ⌃ Pray

Do you have a similar story to tell? The details will be very different, but the essence the same. He called you; you could not help but follow.

Pray for the clarity and simplicity of the response that Levi had. And pray that he would speak the same words to those you know and love who are resisting his call.

## Doctor on call
**Read Luke 5:29-32**

- ❓ *Why are the religious leaders so shocked by Levi's party?*
- ❓ *What does this show about them?*
- ❓ *How does Jesus' answer reveal both their problem and his mission?*

Self-righteousness remains a very modern problem. 40 years ago it was Christians and churches who were accused of being self-righteous hypocrites. And we have much to answer for that. Our churches need to resemble hospital waiting rooms, where we know that we are there for a reason; not smart garden parties where everyone wants to look their best. Today, you can see self-righteous secular preaching everywhere—stand-up comedians, virtue signalling on social media, environmental activists and politicians. Everyone wants to project their "rightness". And many happily bend the truth about themselves to fit in with their internal narrative that *I am right and you are wrong.*

## ⌄ Apply

We have a testimony to share on this. In all humility, we can say that we were, and still are, wrecks on life-support. We desperately needed a doctor to fix us. If you don't think you need forgiveness, if you have convinced yourself that you are truly righteous, then you're not ready to receive Jesus.

# The fast show

*The sparring continues between the Lord and the religious leaders. They are looking to the letter of the law, and do not realise that its fulfilment stands in front of them.*

## A point in time
**Read Luke 5:33-35**

Fasting is seeing a resurgence these days as a dieting trend/fad. But what was the purpose of fasting in the OT law?

Fasting is linked to humbling ourselves before God. Moses fasted on the mountain before he received the Ten Commandments. But fasting is nowhere *explicitly* commanded—except perhaps on the Day of Atonement. Fasting had become, like the ritual washing of hands and pots, part of the religious superstructure that was built in addition to God's clear word.

> ❓ What is good about spiritual fasting, do you think? What are the potential benefits?
> ❓ What is dangerous about fasting?
> ❓ What is the implied criticism in v 33?
> ❓ What is the essence of Jesus' answer?
> ❓ What prediction is hidden in his reply?

Religious people create artificial standards by which we are made right with God—and to judge each other. They thought by doing these things, God would be pleased with them. Of course, fasting as a sign of humbling yourself before God can be a worthwhile discipline; as a way of reminding ourselves that our food comes from God; and that "man shall not live on bread alone". But what they completely missed was the importance of this moment, this person stood

in front of them. God's fulfilment of all he promised in the Old Testament was coming to its conclusion; a fulfilment that would see the end of the sacrificial system as Jesus' perfect sacrifice on the cross was made. This should be a time of joyful celebration.

## Old and new
**Read Luke 5:36-39**

> ❓ What are the three separate word pictures that Jesus paints here?
> ❓ What does each of them mean?
> ❓ How is each of them a challenge to the religious leaders?

Something new has come, and it cannot be contained within the old structures of Old Testament law, and the practices that have grown up around it. But there is also a different criticism in verse 39. Of course, people love the old wine. They will not give up their religious practices so easily. They will continue to view them as better, more valuable, more sophisticated than the rather coarse and unrefined new wine they believe Jesus to be.

## ⌄ Apply

> ❓ What bits of religion are you hanging on to—or do you turn back to—as an alternative to the fresh, effervescent wine of the gospel?

Celebrate with joy the gift of the Bridegroom, who died for his bride, the church.

# Lord of the Sabbath

*The battle between law and grace; old wine and new; religion and Jesus continues, as the Pharisees get more and more agitated by Jesus.*

## Ground rules

### Read Exodus 20:8-11

- ❓ *What were people meant to do on the Sabbath?*
- ❓ *What are the reasons for it? What were God's people supposed to be remembering and celebrating?*
- ❓ *What should be fundamentally joyful about Sabbath-resting?*
- ❓ *How could it so easily lose its connection with the meaning and motivation, and become a ritual and a burden?*
- ❓ *What do you know about the rules and laws that the Pharisees added to the fourth commandment?*

The commandments expressed how the saved people of God should live to reflect the goodness and love of the God who redeemed them from slavery. But by the time of the New Testament (and probably much earlier) the Sabbath had become a burden. If your whole view of God and his commandments was that you needed to keep them perfectly in order to be right with God, then breaking the "rule" was unthinkable. And so an elaborate "hedge" was put around the law: hundreds of rules to prevent the possibility that you might break the law by working on the Sabbath. It completely missed the point.

- ❓ *How can Christians and churches do something similar today?*
- ❓ *How can we resist it?*

## Grinding rules

### Read Luke 6:1-5

- ❓ *Why do the Pharisees object, and why are they wrong?*
- ❓ *What Old Testament precedent does Jesus quote, and what is the hidden claim within it (see 5:34)?*
- ❓ *Why is Jesus' claim in 6:5 so staggering?*

In Exodus we read that "the seventh day is a sabbath to the LORD your God ... the LORD blessed the Sabbath day and made it holy". The day quite literally belongs to God. But his clever wording ("the Son of Man" could be just a man, or refer to Daniel's vision of God's Messiah) teaches two things. First that, as he says elsewhere, "the Sabbath was made for man, not man for the Sabbath" (Mark 2:27-28)—we use it to joyfully rest, refresh and celebrate, not as a burdensome chore and an imposition. Second, it is a direct claim to be God. And Jesus, the Lord of grace, joy, rest, new wine and wedding celebration will inevitably butt heads with the old wine of dead religion.

## ⌄ Apply

- ❓ *What makes you joyful, rested and thankful; what restores your soul?*
- ❓ *Are these the things that you can happily embrace on your Sabbath rest days without guilt? Or are you still drinking the old wine?*

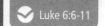
# Withering critique

*The Sabbath-wars continue as Jesus' popularity with the people continues to grow, matched by the hostility of the religious leaders.*

## Put it to the vote
### Read Luke 6:6-11

- ❓ *Why were the scribes and Pharisees listening to Jesus' teaching (v 7)?*
- ❓ *What is at the heart of Jesus' accusation to them in the question of verse 9?*
- ❓ *How would doing this in front of the crowd have incensed the religious leaders even more?*
- ❓ *What Old Testament echoes might this healing have suggested to people?*
- ❓ *What is so wrong about the reaction in verse 11?*

Notice that Jesus simply wants to teach (v 6). It is why he came. But Jesus' teaching about the inappropriate use and misapplication of OT laws had put him on a collision course with those who upheld the system—and presumably also made a living from it.

## Pray

There is an inherent danger in religious leadership. What should be humble, prayerful, self-giving service, can so easily flip to become self-serving, manipulative and damaging. Pray for your leaders, and for those who control the way your church is governed. Ask that they wouldn't give in to any of these temptations, but would be caring shepherds like the Lord Jesus.

## Apply

- ❓ *What fundamental error had the religious leaders fallen into (v 9)?*
- ❓ *How might we fall into the same trap today?*

When rules are disconnected from their meaning and purpose, you end up with dead religion that serves itself and is manipulative and damaging to those it claims to be serving. This is not the way of Jesus. The furious reaction of the leaders illustrates yet again how the darkness hates the light that exposes it; especially when Jesus calls out their hypocrisy in front of the people they are both repressing and living off.

But this raises the question: if the leaders of God's people—both political and religious—were so badly compromised, if the law had lost its purpose, if the new wine of God's kingdom was coming—then perhaps it was time to appoint new leaders, to articulate new laws that encapsulated the true meaning of God's law. This is exactly what Jesus does next.

## Pray

Ask God to give you leaders like his Son: people who long to do good and to save lives as they teach the good news rather than destroy (v 9).

# The sermon on the plain

*Over the next two weeks we'll really get into this great sermon—very similar to the Sermon on the Mount (Matthew 5 – 7) yet with some striking emphases of its own.*

## A symbolic occasion

**Read Luke 6:12-19**

❓ *What are the signs that this was a special occasion?*

❓ *What do the signs suggest Jesus was doing?*

Jesus prays up the mountain prior to choosing "The Twelve"—the number twelve is significant. This is the twelve tribes of Israel being set up anew. Jesus mirrors Moses, who came down the mountain with the law (Exodus 20). Jesus is about to present to us his new law for the new covenant.

Just as the giving of the law on Mount Sinai was accompanied by lightning and earthquakes, the healings and exorcisms act to show the importance and significance of what follows.

People were queuing up to be healed but Jesus' priority is to proclaim his new law.

## Why God gives laws

The Bible tells us that God's law is a light (Psalm 119:105; Proverbs 6:23) that shows us our true selves. But let's be clear—we don't become God's people by obeying the law. That always happens by God's grace and rescue. But the law shows us that we *need* God's rescue and forgiveness. It is the mirror showing our need of a wash rather than the soap that washes us clean.

*The law shows us our path.* Once we are forgiven, Jesus shows us the way to live. And live well! The repetition of "blessed" in what follows emphasises that God is no killjoy. Walking his path always means blessing.

*The law shows us our weakness.* This is the path of blessing but not of ease. We will be utterly unable to walk it without the constant help of the Holy Spirit.

*The law shows the way for those who are not yet believers.* Many who weren't yet disciples were listening in (Luke 6:17-19). Jesus shines his light down his path so all may know what it will mean to follow him.

We often think of law as the downside of the Bible but the old Puritans used to speak of the "grace of law". In all the ways above the Lord Jesus has been gracious in giving us his law.

## ⌄ Apply

Jesus' disciples were chosen to be people-fishers. But hand in hand with this, they need to discover what it means to live the truly blessed life. A big part of people-fishing is showing how wonderful life is under the rule of the Lord Jesus.

❓ *How is your life doing so? Does anything need to change?*

# Christian counter-culture

*Before looking at the individual "trees" of these verses one by one, we'll look at the "wood" of the whole passage, to see some important perspectives.*

## Counter-cultural

**Read Luke 6:20-26**

Look at the two lists of blessings and woes.

- ❓ *Which would our world label woe and blessing?*
- ❓ *How does that compare with what Jesus is saying?*

You see the point? The law of Christ is not intuitive. It turns the values of the world upside down—or rather the right way up. The world's cultures may vary in many ways, but they all have this in common—they are the opposite way round to the law of Christ.

## Counter-intuitive

Jesus' words are startling.

- ❓ *Why was he so provocative—especially to his own disciples?*

My computer has a default setting to which it returns whenever I try and change it. Our default position (our natural and overriding instinct), even when we are disciples, is to see life the opposite way round to Jesus. So he uses shock tactics to swing his disciples around the right way.

## Counter-comfort

- ❓ *What will following Christ do to your life—in the short-term at least?*

Jesus makes it clear that following him will affect your life. You *cannot* be a Christian in theory. Discipleship is not just knowing that he leads us against the flow; it is following him—into poverty, hunger, even weeping (v 20-22).

It has been said that faith could be spelled R. I. S. K. Living all out for Jesus feels like stepping off the dry land of solid human experience and trying to walk on water. Sounds pretty foolish, doesn't it? And yet a Christian is someone who is convinced that it is never foolish to take any risk with Jesus, but rather, the really risky thing is to ignore him and to go our own way.

## ☑ Apply

- ❓ *Are God's blessings different from your ideas of happiness?*
- ❓ *Are you ready to follow Jesus against the flow of your culture and its values?*
- ❓ *Where do you think the particular pressure points are at the moment?*

It's easy to default to thinking we must fight the world on issues of social morality. But the call here is to, first and foremost, grow a Christ-like character in ourselves.

Pray now that you would discover what it truly means to live the blessed life over the next two weeks.

# He has done it!

*Despite the blackness, silence and pain, Jesus' hope in his Father's promise is well founded: suffering and death are not the end, but the door to eternal life.*

Jesus' resurrection is the great "Yes" of God to his sacrificial self-offering.

## Vindicated

### Read Psalm 22:22-24

❓ *What are we being called to do? Why?*

Hebrews 2:10-12 quotes verse 22, saying that Jesus' suffering makes him the perfect and acceptable sacrifice for sin. The result: many sons are brought to glory—whom the Lord Jesus is pleased to call "family".

## ⌄ Apply

When we meet with other Christians, when we talk with family, friends, neighbours and strangers, our duty and our joy will be to declare the name of Jesus to them and praise God for all he has done in and through him for us.

## A joyful response

### Read Psalm 22:25-31

❓ *Who will benefit from the suffering Saviour?*

The one who has been delivered will rejoice, and many others will see the benefits of this deliverance:

- The poor (v 26a): a Bible term for those who humble themselves before God. Their fortunes are reversed, and they enjoy a life of wealth and satisfaction. See Matthew 5:3; Luke 1:53.
- The seekers (Psalm 22:26): there is now an answer to their questions about God, love and the meaning of life.
- The world (v 27): before, salvation was only to be found in Israel, and among a few fortunate outsiders. Jesus' death and resurrection open the gates of salvation to the whole world.
- The rich (v 29): not just the lowly poor, but also the good and the great will be gathered in.
- The dead (v 29b): he is the God of "the living and the dead" and proves to be the Saviour of the faithful—even those who lived before he came.
- The future generations(v 30, 31): The good news of salvation through Christ applies not only to the past, but also to future generations, who will hear the message.

## ⌄ Apply

The message is for *everybody*: those you meet in the street or on the bus next to you, the people at work, the shop assistant or waiter that serves you, the delivery guy and the bin men, the Afghan and Argentinian, the refugee and the managing director, the crowd of noisy kids in the street, the baby in your arms, the senior citizen, the people next door, and the people on TV.

❓ *The fulfillment of verse 31 is in your hands. What are you going to do?*

# The genuine article?

*We love to be positive. But every positive benefit of following Christ carries with it a negative implication that we sometimes find hard to talk about.*

## Woes

**Read Luke 6:20-26 and also Matthew 5:1-12**

❓ *What is the most obvious difference between the two sermons?*

❓ *Why do you think Jesus preaches "woes" as well as blessings in his Luke sermon?*

Jesus only *implies* the negatives in Matthew (though Matthew records much more explicit woes in chapter 23). But in his Luke sermon, Jesus puts the two bang next door to each other. He drives home this fact—the world is divided very clearly into two camps. Jesus divides *everyone* into those who will receive blessing and those who will get nothing but woe.

## ☑ Apply

We get used to "dialling down the dark side" of the gospel message. Yes, salvation is freely on offer and it's wonderful. But there is a horrific cost to rejecting Jesus that we need, in some way, at some stage, to articulate clearly to our friends.

❓ *Are you guilty of ignoring this part of Jesus' message?*

❓ *How would you go about telling someone about the serious consequences of rejecting Christ?*

❓ *Is there someone you need to have this conversation with soon?*

## Drawing the line

❓ *What actually is the dividing line between the two groups?*

❓ *Notice again to whom Jesus is speaking. Do the disciples get the blessings while the others get the woes? Or is it more complicated than that?*

In fact, Jesus proclaims both blessings and woes to his disciples (Luke 6:20)! They could still get woe. Of course, the crowd is also listening in (v 17- 19) and since they haven't yet committed to following Jesus, they are in danger of ending up in the group that inherits woe for certain. Even so, Jesus' words, which are directed to his disciples, are a clear warning to each of us. What matters is the life of discipleship, not just membership of the discipleship club.

## ☑ Apply

So, what about us? Are we true disciples or false ones? Genuine or fake? Some would doubt whether we should ask ourselves this at all. After all, doesn't the gospel tell us that forgiveness is a free gift, and therefore our salvation is completely sure? Absolutely! (See Luke 18:9-14; 19:1-10) And yet we are also called to test ourselves "to see whether you are in the faith" (2 Corinthians 13:5).

And the test? Shockingly—it seems to be whether we are rich or poor, hungry or filled... More on this in the next study.

# Circumstances matter

*We continue our overview of the basic ideas of the Beatitudes, and the many challenges they contain to how we think and live.*

**Read Luke 6:20-26 and also Matthew 5:1-12**

Look at the things that make someone blessed in Matthew and in Luke.

## What is the difference?

The Victorian preacher J.C. Ryle put it like this: "In Matthew the point brought forward in each case is the spiritual character of the person, in St Luke his temporal circumstances and condition".

Of course, character and circumstances are connected. When Jesus says in Luke that the "poor" and "hungry" are blessed he clearly does not mean that people have the kingdom of God merely by having nothing in their pockets or on their plates. He means "poor" because Christian— or perhaps Christian because "poor". He is really still interested in our spiritual character.

But, whereas in Matthew Jesus goes straight for the attitude, in Luke he underlines circumstances to show how much they can affect our character. It is as if he is saying, *You may think it is easy to have comfortable circumstances and the right spiritual attitude, but actually that is unlikely.* Typically it is the "poor" who are "poor in spirit" (humble and dependent on God).

And the rest of Scripture agrees. We are more likely to see our need of God if we are "badly-off" here; more likely to be proud

and self-sufficient if we are well-off. (See Isaiah 61:1; Luke 4:18-19; 14:15-24.)

Jesus became poor for our sake (2 Corinthians 8:9). He put God's will and our salvation before any earthly success he could have achieved. And he is our pattern (Luke 9:23-27). God typically chooses those in "mean circumstances" (1 Corinthians 1:26) so that "no one may boast before him" (v 29). No one may think they can impress their way into God's kingdom. Living a Christian life is liable to be bad for our circumstances here. That is not always the case—but in the New Testament it is often so (see Hebrews 10:32-34).

## Apply

**?** *Why is it that good circumstances seem so important to us?*

**?** *Why do we default to thinking that this earth seems to be all there is?*

**?** *Do we think we can develop a godly character irrespective of our circumstances?*

**?** *Do we think God is really on the side of the impressive and substantial?*

## Pray

Talk to God about the impact of this general principle. And invite God's Spirit to search your heart for wrong ideas, and replace them with the ones that truly please him.

# It's good to be poor

*What is Jesus saying about poverty? That it's a good thing? Really? For most of us, falling into poverty, after ill health, is perhaps the worst thing we can imagine.*

## How poor?
### Read Luke 6:20 and 18:18-30

Luke brings out a strand of Jesus' teaching which particularly distrusts material wealth. Jesus shows that material poverty is not the worst fate that can befall us.

···· TIME OUT ·····································

If you have time, follow through this strand of the Lord's teaching on wealth in this Gospel by reading Luke 12:13-34; 14:15-24; 16:10-15, 16:19-31; 19:1-10.

·····································

- ❷ *So what does Jesus mean in Luke 6:20?*
- ❷ *What do you think he doesn't mean?*
- ❷ *What are your reactions to this statement?*

It's not that being poor automatically qualifies us for heaven (see yesterday). Neither that being poor is easy to cope with. Jesus was realistic about this (see Luke 16:19-21). There is nothing good about poverty itself. Christianity is not masochism. It's not that being poor always leads us to God—we know that is not the case. It's not that we should make no efforts to earn a living and provide for our families (see 1 Thessalonians 4:11-12).

But we should note this: being poor is not the worst thing in the world. Far better to have the kingdom of God and be poor than be rich without God! And remember

yesterday? Poverty is much more likely than riches to go with genuine Christian faith.

Imagine there is a spectrum of opinion on the subject of material wealth like this:

$$\longleftrightarrow$$

*Poverty is bad*        *Riches are bad*

- ❷ *Where would your view be on this line?*
- ❷ *Where do you think Jesus would end up?*

Of course, it is much more nuanced than this, but we mustn't argue ourselves out of the fundamental challenge Jesus poses to us here. That would be to join the party of the Pharisees. Surely Jesus would be towards the right (even if not quite at the end)—whereas we tend to be towards the other end (even if not quite there).

## ☑ Apply

- ❷ *In your ambitions and financial goals do you aim to earn a "living wage" so that you can further your service of the Lord—or to get as far away from poverty as possible?*
- ❷ *Are you "poor" enough to look forward to Jesus returning and taking you to the riches of heaven?*
- ❷ *What in your life are you prepared (or not prepared) to reorganise so as to live the way Jesus wants?*

# You'll be laughing!

*Jesus wants us to be under no illusions. Living as a disciple will be tough. But how does Jesus equip his disciples to keep going through hunger and sorrow?*

## Hope
**Read Luke 6:20-21**

- ❓ *What is it that sets us free from caring about food and possessions here?*
- ❓ *What is it that will enable us to be free from being driven by our inner hungers?*

The focus here is seeing the future clearly. Only by understanding—by faith—what the future holds will we understand what truly matters now. The gospel promise is that we will have far greater riches then, and so if we set our hearts and minds on the things ahead, our attitude towards money, possessions, wealth and all that goes with it will be dialled right back.

## Satisfaction
**Read Isaiah 55:1-2 and Romans 8:18-25**

- ❓ *What picture of our future do these verses reveal to us?*

Heaven will be a feast and full of the richest of fare. These verses speak of soul satisfaction—but also bodily redemption. All wrong yearnings will be gone. All right yearnings will be totally satisfied.

## ☑ Apply

Lots of people have "bucket lists"—things they would love to do before they die. They save and spend to travel or own a painting or now, visit space. Believers know that we will have all these things and more in the new creation.

- ❓ *So what should a Christian "bucket list" look like?*

## Laughter
**Read Isaiah 55:12**

Here is a picture of total and exuberant joy—hearts thrilled and filled to overflowing. It is no surprise, then, that Jesus depicted heaven as a great banquet. He wants us to be absolutely clear that it will be wonderful beyond our imagination.

## ☑ Apply

The 17th-century Puritan Richard Baxter used to spend half an hour meditating on heaven every morning. No doubt that kept him going through the terms of imprisonment that he suffered for Christ and also during his continual illnesses.

Why not try something similar? How about these questions for starters?

- ❓ *What present troubles from my own life am I looking forward to being rid of in heaven?*
- ❓ *What troubles in the world at large am I looking forward to being absent in the new creation?*
- ❓ *What particular delights am I longing for in heaven? See Revelation 21:1-4, 22-27 if you need help.*

*Bible in a year: Job 32-33 • 1 Corinthians 11:1-16* ✔

# Leaping for joy

*We love to be loved. It is a rare person who is happy to embrace the hatred and derision of others. Those who do so must have a strong reason...*

## Realistic

Skim back over Luke's Gospel so far.

> ❷ *What signs of hatred for Jesus and his disciples have we seen?*

**Read Luke 6:22**

> ❷ *How will people typically respond to Jesus' followers?*
> ❷ *Will it be fair?*
> ❷ *Where will persecution come from? (What hint is given in the reference to mistreating the prophets, v 23?)*

Note Jesus' realism. He wants his followers to know that persecution will be part of the normal Christian life. You can see this foreshadowed already in Luke (6:11 for example). Jesus frequently warned of the same thing elsewhere (e.g. 9:23-27).

The experience of the New Testament church bears out Jesus' warning (e.g. Acts 4:1-22; 5:17-42). And no—it will not be fair. We will be called evil. And note—it won't just be the irreligious; the Pharisees had already led the opposition to Jesus. There will be much persecution in the name of God. And—all that will be extremely hurtful.

## Rejoicing

**Read Luke 6:23**

> ❷ *But in the face of all this, how should Christians respond?*
> ❷ *What is the reason for this?*

This really is Jesus turning the world upside down. We are to rejoice when we are rejected for his sake. Jesus says we should rejoice because our rejection shows that we are genuine. We stand in the line of God's prophets of old. And the extraordinary thing is that the first believers actually did rejoice! (Read Acts 5:40-42.)

Jesus isn't saying that persecution is not horrible. He surely wouldn't have agreed that *ills have no weight and tears no bitterness* (that's a line from the hymn *Abide with Me*), having just said: "Blessed are you who weep". Some young student missionaries to France, from 16th-century Geneva, wrote joyfully from prison (where their life expectancy was about six months) that they found themselves in "the true school of Christ".

## ⌃ Pray

How about this for a prayer? Not just that we would persevere when persecution comes—but that we would rejoice!

Pray for Christians worldwide who face far harsher rejection and persecution than those of us in Western democracies. Pray that they would be filled with joyful laughter as they think about their heavenly reward.

# Well-off tell-off

*Ok. So most of us are relatively well-off. But what does that mean for my relationship with God? Is it in danger because of my bank balance?*

**Read Luke 6:24**

❓ *What is your immediate, visceral response to what Jesus says?*
❓ *What questions does it raise in your mind?*

## ⌃ Pray

Swearing, lying, drunkenness, sexual sins. Of course, all of us are capable of these things. But, in Christian circles, they are un-acceptable— wouldn't you agree? However, when it comes to materialism, we comfortably fall into feeling that it is acceptable— so much part of the very air of this world that it has seeped quite unnoticed into the church. Pray right now, as you read these verses, for eyes to see materialism for what it really is—evil.

## So—what to do?

**Read Luke 12:13-34**

❓ *What is the problem with storing up earthly riches?*
❓ *And what is the solution?*

It's important to say that the poor can also be materialistic. And also that having riches does not prevent real repentance (see the example of Zacchaeus in 19:1-10)—although often it does. Jesus' point is that earthly riches just don't last.

## ⌄ Apply

We start by meditating on heaven (6:21), but it's more than that. The answer comes in 12:33-34. Note especially the wording of verse 34. Jesus does not say *Where your heart is, your treasure will be also.* He says the opposite. It is easy to think that *longing* for heaven will lead to *living* for heaven. But Jesus says that *living* for heaven will lead to *longing* for heaven.

Invest in heaven and you will want to be there. Put your treasure there and you will long to be there.

❓ *So—when did you last "sell your possessions" (or not buy something) and give to the poor or give to the work of the gospel, for that matter?*

Jesus' words are crystal clear. He certainly does not command us to sell all our possessions—we should have enough to live on. But he does tell us to invest as much as we can in heaven. So what's our response? Give what we can and keep what we have to? No!—we need to give what we have to and keep what we can. We tend to do things completely the wrong way round! The air of materialism has got into all of us, and we need to take hold of ourselves firmly to free ourselves from it.

Talk to God now about your fundamental attitude towards your wealth.

# A long time crying

*Time is not just relative in the sense that Einstein observed. It is relative in our experience. Hours and years seem to pass very quickly, or moments stretch on slowly.*

## Relative time

### Read Luke 6:25

- ❓ *What is the "shelf life" of earthly laughter (in the context of v 20-26)?*
- ❓ *And how long will hunger and weeping last?*
- ❓ *What appalling realisation does Jesus want us to imagine and prepare for?*

In the passage as a whole, Jesus contrasts a short time on earth with eternity (v 23). And he wants his hearers to taste something of how dreadful it will be for people to realise that they have had all the comfort and joy they will ever, ever have.

A friend insisted to me that the God of the Old Testament is harsh and vengeful, whereas Jesus is loving and forgiving. And, of course, it is true that the gospel of grace is seen with far greater clarity in the New than the Old Testament. And yet Jesus also warned more about hell than anyone else in the New Testament. Look again at verse 25.

- ❓ *What does this hunger and weeping stand for?*

Hunger stands for our deepest longings. Saying for ever, *If only I had truly turned to Christ.* Mourning and weeping stand for a misery in which there is no good thing, no mitigating circumstance, no friendship, no warmth, no hope.

## ✅ Apply

Some people say that we should not explicitly teach these things and so dangle people over hell because it puts them under unfair emotional pressure. There may be an element of truth in that. But which is ultimately more dangerous—pressurising people or leaving them unwarned? Rather, let's ask how we can warn them more effectively and with more care.

Others say that we should not become Christians just to escape hell because conversion becomes unworthy self-preservation. But Jesus thought otherwise—and sin is distrusting him—even if it seems selfish.

Or perhaps Christians need never think about hell again—as we have been totally forgiven (Romans 8:1). Yet, John Wesley always remembered that he was "a brand plucked from the burning"—that is, he never forgot he was a hell-bound sinner who had been quite amazingly saved.

## ⌃ Pray

Praise God that you too are "a brand plucked from the burning".

Pray for family, friends, colleagues and neighbours who stand on the brink of the abyss. And pray for opportunities to share the good news.

# People pleasers

*We've already seen that we are inveterate people pleasers. What Jesus says next digs deep into that instinct with a powerful challenge.*

**Read Luke 6:26**

❓ *What sort of approval does Jesus warn against (compare with v 22-23)?*
❓ *What basic human weakness does Jesus highlight?*

Jesus warns against the temptation to be popular with people. It is more attractive to us than our relationship with God, and therefore becomes more valued. Particularly, he is warning against the temptation to tone down God's word, in order to be well-thought of in religious circles. False prophets will *always* be popular because they say what people want to hear (see Jeremiah 8:11; 2 Timothy 4:3).

According to Jesus, if you are popular, it suggests that you are heading for hell—because it shows that you prefer the praise of people to that of God.

## The Biblical balance

How does the rest of Scripture speak to this question? Below is a summary:

- Luke 2:52: favour with people is not wrong—though note the order of "God" and "man" in the verse.

- Matthew 5:9; Romans 12:18: we are commanded to be peacemakers and live at peace with everyone.

- Philippians 4:2-3; Titus 3:9-11: we are forbidden to be divisive and argumentative within the church.

And yet even when things appear to be going smoothly and well, there is a warning: "Woe to you when everyone speaks well of you".

## The Biblical priority

Part of Jesus' point is that we must get our priorities right. When it comes to a choice between popularity with people and with God—there can be no contest (e.g. Galatians 1:10).

## The Biblical motive

Jesus also highlights our motivation—it is *to please God*. We would search Scripture fruitlessly for any command to "please" fellow humans. Sometimes pleasing God will lead to favour with others (Luke 2:52), sometimes it will not (see 9:21-27).

All of us want to please people at some level. For some it is personal popularity that matters while others care more for public reputation— the difference between *I want to feel liked* and *I want to feel respected*. But, sometimes at least, Jesus will lead us out of both and into unpopularity.

❓ *Who actually disapproves of you for your Christian faith?*
❓ *In your heart of hearts whom do you actually want to please?*

Talk to the Lord about your answers.

# Enemy love

*So far in this sermon, Jesus has proclaimed that the world is standing on its head. What the world means by well-off and badly-off is upside down.*

He has ended the first part of the sermon with some words on how rightly to relate to others—we are not to be governed by what pleases them (v 26). Now, in the second part, he continues with the subject of other people and how to relate to them. We are not to seek to please them—but we are to love them.

## Mercy mindset

**Read Luke 6:27-28**

- ❓ *What does genuine love for enemies look like?*
- ❓ *From the context, who is it that is doing the persecuting and abusing?*
- ❓ *Why do you think that these counter-intuitive commands are part of Jesus' way of living?*

Mercy seems to be the running theme here—love like that of the merciful God, not the merciless world. We've moved into part two of Jesus' sermon only to find the same counter-culture message.

**Re-read Luke 6:27**

- ❓ *How does this verse relate to the following verse?*
- ❓ *What is the shock ingredient?*
- ❓ *How exactly is Jesus different from the world?*

Verse 27 spells out the principle on which verses 28-31 expand. And the shock ingredient is—*enemies!* All humans know about love—and almost all approve of it. But as humans we love those who love us or are loveable to us—tit-for-tat love. Whereas Jesus preached "enemy love".

## ☑ Apply

It's crucial to get practical with this.

- ❓ *Think of some people who have personally wronged you, or who you instinctively dislike. Read the verses again, substituting their names. How does this make you feel?*
- ❓ *When did you last deliberately do good to someone who hated you (for your faith or otherwise)?*
- ❓ *When did you last pray for someone who ill-treated you?*

Christians are called, not only to receive mercy, but also to pass on mercy. It could be described as a sort of "holy infection" of enemy love. We do not have it in our natural state, but we catch it from Christ, and then it infects our whole attitude to other people

## ⌃ Pray

Now would be a good time to put this into practice. Pray for someone who you count as an enemy.

And ask God for the strength—that comes from the knowledge of his grace towards you—to go on loving them.

*Bible in a year: Proverbs 1-2 • 1 Corinthians 14:21-40*

# Retaliating rightly

*Jesus gets more concrete in this verse. "Enemy love" is to be lived out in flesh and bone—even in bruised flesh and bone.*

**Read Luke 6:27-31**

In verse 29 Jesus is possibly referring to a ritual slap given to Christian "heretics" in the synagogue—but surely this command need not be limited to that.

❓ *When assaulted, what should a Christian resist doing?*

❓ *When assaulted, how should a Christian react?*

We are not to resist our attacker and—much harder—we must resist our tendency to fight back. In fact, we are to leave ourselves open to further ill-treatment.

## Hard examples

A host of "buts" shoot into our minds with verses like this. *But—what about burglars, domestic abuse, rapists, Hitler?* Let's think through several points.

*The type of Scripture.* J.C. Ryle points out that in these verses we have "strong proverbial forms of expressing a great principle". That is, Jesus intends to make one point strongly rather than say everything on the subject. The rest of Scripture has other things to say.

*The immediate context.* Jesus is not addressing the issue of defending someone, nor even reasonable self-defence, nor gracious protest over wrong done to us. He is saying, *Do not follow your natural taste for retaliation/revenge—and do not use force to get what you want.*

*The rest of Scripture.* The God-given role of governments is to use force against evil (see Romans 13:4). But here in Luke and also in Matthew 5:38-42 Jesus addresses individuals. John Stott comments, "Jesus was not prohibiting the administration of justice, but rather forbidding us to take the law into our own hands".

So, Paul insisted on justice (see Acts 16:37). He wanted to preserve the rule of law. There's no problem with calling the police for a burglar, or reporting abuse of any kind to the authorities. More than that, it is our God-ordained duty to do this. God will deal with these people through the system he has ordained and set in place. And yet—there is to be no hint of vengeance and retaliation in us.

## ⌄ Apply

❓ *Driving: are you responding with aggression or mercy?*

❓ *Relationships: are you using force to get what you want—physical or emotional?*

❓ *Are you the object of persecution or injustice:? Are you responding with prayer, kind speech, doing good, or are you raging with anger?*

❓ *Can you extend the list or make it more specific to you?*

Remind yourself of the mercy of God towards you as you wrestle with perhaps complex emotions on this subject.

*Bible in a year: Proverbs 3-5 • 1 Corinthians 15:1-28*

# Possessiveness prohibited

*Jesus continues in the same vein as before but moves from attacks on our person to attacks on our property.*

## Cloak donations

**Read Luke 6:29b-30**

❷ *What situations does Jesus envisage?*
❷ *What must we resist?*
❷ *What must we do instead?*

Clearly, the world lives by a code which says it is more important to protect property than to bless others. However, Jesus says that blessing others is a much higher priority—and that includes blessing those who want to relieve us of our property by stealing or by begging.

## More hard examples

Remember—one point is being made strongly. As we have already seen, this is not everything the Bible has to say on the subject, so we need to note the following:

- It is not necessarily saying that we should refrain from calling the police when robbed (Romans 13:4 again). The good of society does matter—it is right that criminals are brought to justice through the system.

- It is not saying that there is no limit on how much we should give (see 2 Corinthians 8:13-15).

- It is not saying that we shouldn't exercise discretion about who to give to. This is not a mandate for wasting money by giving it to be spent on drink or on charities/

causes which, according to the Bible, are wrong or pointless, or which are corrupt or inefficient (see 2 Thessalonians 3:10-12; 1 Timothy 5:3, 9-10).

What it is saying:

- We should have *absolutely no possessiveness*. Possessiveness should never determine what we give or what we allow people to take. Far better to live for blessing others and risk losing possessions than to live only for material things. After all, surely Jesus would ask: *Don't you trust God to provide for you* (Luke 12:22-30)?

## ☑ Apply

❷ *We need to think hard about how to live this out. How would you approach the following situations?*
- *You are robbed in the street.*
- *Your neighbour tries to annex a foot or two of your garden.*
- *A visitor to your house takes some money and you know who has done it.*
- *A friend (Christian or not-Christian) borrows some money and fails to return it (1 Corinthians 6:1-8 may help here).*

Today would be a great day to engage with other Christians on this question. If you're part of the Explore Facebook page why not start a discussion about it?

*facebook.com/groups/tgbc.explore*

# Positive love

*This is a version of what is generally known as the "Golden Rule". "I'll scratch your back if you scratch mine"? Is that what Jesus is saying?*

## Pure gold

**Read Luke 6:31**

❓ *What does Jesus want us to imagine— and then do?*

There were similar sayings among the Jews and Greeks throughout the ancient world. The Greeks, though, usually took it to recommend mutual back-scratching or revenge, *Do to others as they do to you.* Jesus clearly does not mean that. Nor is it "Do to others *so that* they will do to you". Rather, verse 31 comes in the context of "enemy love" which leaves us open to further slaps and stealing. Jewish rabbis wrote about its negative form: *Don't do to others*—which gets pretty close to our contemporary saying "Live and let live".

By making it positive, Jesus is not just *slightly* changing things. His way is totally different—a call to overflowing positive love in action.

## ☑ Apply

We've now come to the end of this chunk of studies in this challenging section. Look back on the sermon so far.

❓ *What have been the running themes?*
❓ *What has most struck you?*

## Jesus' law

Jesus has called us to see that reality is his way—the opposite of the world's way—and

to live accordingly. The problem is that we fail continually to live his way. So let's end by reminding ourselves what Jesus' law is for and praying accordingly.

- *It shows us ourselves.* Jesus doesn't address the question of how we become acceptable to God. That always happens by God's rescue and grace rather than obeying the law. But one main purpose of the law is to send us back to the cross for fresh forgiveness. Pray to him for that instinct.

- *It shows us our path.* Christ's law sends us to Christ to be forgiven—and then shows us the way forgiven people must live. Yet we desperately need the strength of his Holy Spirit if we are to do so. We cannot do this ourselves. Let's cry to him for that strength and empowerment.

- *It shows the way for those who are not yet Christians.* Jesus shines his light down the path of discipleship so all may know what it will mean to follow him. Pray that those you love would have these things revealed to them.

## ☑ Pray

Spend some time remembering and giving thanks for people who have treated you with mercy, generosity, kindness—perhaps quite undeserved.

Now think how you might "do to others" in the same way, and pray for the opportunity.

*Bible in a year: Proverbs 8 • 1 Corinthians 16:1-9*

# Who looks after me?

*It's worth slowing down and drinking in with care the 6 verses of the most famous song in history.*

Shepherd boy David looks out over the flocks under his charge. For these he is responsible; for these he is accountable. Their hunger, thirst and well-being are his constant concern.

You can almost hear him asking: *But who cares for me? I look ahead for food, water, safety and shelter. But doesn't the shepherd also need a shepherd? I look after them; but who looks after me?* The answer that formed in the mind of this king-in-the-making is nothing less than a revelation...

## The Lord is my shepherd
### Read Psalm 23:1-6

❷ *What's his answer to that question?*

Revelation—God's word written down for us—is special because it changes not just one person's perception of God, but *everyone's* perception of God. You cannot read this and see God in the same way again.

Were it not in the Bible, even Christians might be offended at this portrayal of God in such a down-to-earth and ordinary fashion. While "religion" seems to spend its time making God a distant abstract idea, Christianity declares our God to be close, real, involved and reachable.

···· TIME OUT ·····

David's reflection on his own job brought him a wonderful insight into the character and ways of God and his relationship with

us. If you are a doctor or health worker, you might realise the value of Jesus being the "Great Physician" (Mark 2:17). Everything you strive to do for your patients, might then illustrate more clearly the far more perfect skill and care of God for us.

❷ *Is there something about your own job that can teach you something about God and his relationship to you that you have not seen before?*

## I lack nothing
### Re-read Psalm 23:1

❷ *How does he reach this conclusion?*

For a man who knew what it was to be on Saul's personal "hit list" and to be forced to live on the run and in exile, David's conclusion is a breathtaking one. If the Lord is his shepherd, he will have everything he needs.

## ⌃ Pray

We perhaps find this the most difficult thing to truly believe. Advertisers strive to convince us that we "need" whatever they are selling. Hear the challenge of this simple but devastating verse. In the Shepherd, *you have everything you need.*

Talk to him now and tell him how grateful you are for the way he has met your needs so far in life—and will for ever.

❤ *Bible in a year: Proverbs 9 • 1 Corinthians 16:10-24*

# A bit of a lie down

*We live in a world filled with frenzied activity. Driven by deadlines: the next project, the next target, the next appointment. How do we cope with such stress?*

The human soul is a surprisingly sturdy creation and none of this would matter; except that now, the unending pace and the constant demands have crept into our spirits, and many find it harder and harder to make time and opportunity for feeding our inner lives.

**Read Psalm 23:2**

❓ *What do you think green pastures is a picture of for David?*
❓ *What is the comparable thing for you?*

A flock of well-fed sheep are a credit to the skill and attention of the shepherd as he alternates between the long trail and the hard climb to find the place where the best grass grows and the sheep can feed and feed again.

## ✔ Apply

❓ *How does the Good Shepherd provide for feeding the soul, so we can grow strong in God?*

Could you make a list of the things God uses to feed the life of Jesus in us? How many of them can be "eaten on the run"? If regular meals and a balanced diet are good for our physical well-being, could you plan a healthier diet for your soul from the list you have created? Try reading Acts 2:42 if you're stuck for ideas.

## Beside quiet waters
**Re-read Psalm 23:2**

Sheep can't drink just anywhere. The tumbling waterfall and the swift torrent promise refreshment for their thirst, but are also a threat to their safety. So the shepherd leads them to the quiet waters, where they can drink safely and be satisfied.

But it's not just making space in our busyness by being quiet, or withdrawing and shutting the door. As valuable as these things may be for our sense of peace, what matters more is that we are drinking "the right stuff". **Read John 7:37-39** to discover what this is.

## ^ Pray

There is something about the restless craving of our age—always drinking and never satisfied—that this Scripture speaks powerfully to. The generation that proclaims it no longer has any need of God, proves otherwise by continually searching for a replacement, but never finding anything better. We can deny it; but the thirst will keep coming back and nothing else will satisfy it but God himself.

❓ *Are you looking to something else, or someone else, to fill the place in your life that only Christ truly can?*

Talk to God about your answer.

# A shepherd's care

*No matter how carefully the shepherd chooses the path, the sheep will inevitably suffer the wear and tear of the journey.*

## Soul refreshment

### Read Psalm 23:3

❓ *How would you describe the state of your soul at the moment?*

❓ *What would refreshment look like for you?*

The shepherd goes through the flock, picking out those most in need, and uses his skill to mend their cuts and bruises. We have a shepherd who does a greater thing for our souls. Life is sometimes a bruising contest and, in our progress through it, we too accumulate scratches and even injuries. We need to spend time with the Shepherd so he can restore our souls.

## 🔺 Pray

❓ *What specific things can you identify which have come into your life as you have followed Jesus, which have eaten away at your joy in the Lord?*

Perhaps a setback in business or a difficult period in a relationship has brought a wound into your spirit. Take time now to let the great Shepherd bring healing and restoration, making you whole for the journey ahead.

## The right paths

❓ *What is your experience of God's guidance in everyday life?*

❓ *What specific promise is given here?*

He *will* guide us! It's unconditional, and a reality, whether we see it or not. But God has a higher ambition for our lives than we do. We want to get to the next place. He wants us to be ready for the next place. So he doesn't just pick out any path for us to travel. He picks the one designed to change us as we walk it. Paths of righteousness are not always the easiest, or the quickest, but they are the ones which take us closer to him— because that is our true destination.

## For his name's sake

❓ *If people know you are a follower of Christ, what impression do you hope they receive about Christ by the way you live? What do they actually get?*

What I do may not appear significant, but what I am means a great deal more. When you become a Christian, you become part of a great family who bear the name of Christ. This is an immense privilege for us. But it also means that, as the shepherd is known to the flock that carries his name, so God is shown to others by those who follow him.

## 🔺 Pray

*Lord, I don't understand how following this path will bring me closer to you. But I pray that you will use its difficulties and challenges to make me more like you, more worthy to bear your name.*

# The valley of shadows

*Even those who lead the most charmed of lives in the sunlit uplands will inevitably face shadowy valleys as time and age take their toll on family, friends and their own bodies.*

## The path

**Read Psalm 23:4**

- ❓ What do you think is to be feared in the darkest valley for David as shepherd?
- ❓ What dark valleys have you already been through, or are currently in?
- ❓ What dark valleys await you in the future?
- ❓ What comfort does David find in all of this?

Grief, illness, disappointment, loss—any one of these can suddenly crowd into our life and cast us into darkness. But the very shadow thrown over us is the proof that the light still shines elsewhere. This is not the darkness of the sun gone down, for the shepherd is right there with us.

## No fear

Fear isn't always bad. It teaches us not to argue with the laws of gravity or the destructive power of fire. But fear can also be destructive. Yet it is often not so much what happens to us, but its consequences, that we fear most. Serious illness is a fearful thing; but it is the consequences it brings which are often the real focus of our fear—limitation, restriction, pain, loss of independence, and so on. God does not guarantee we will not have to taste these bitter pills in life. But the worst consequences of illness cannot rob us of our greatest strength, or our greatest prize.

- ❓ Why?
- ❓ How can the "darkest valley" be different when you walk it with God?

## The comfort sticks

- ❓ What do the rod and staff symbolise?
- ❓ How have you seen God use both in your life at different times?

For us, the words are softened by familiarity and distance. The shepherd's rod and staff were tools of the trade. They speak of both rescue and defence from danger. The crook of the staff lifted many a sheep from the awkward position their inability to see danger had put themselves in. The rod was something else. A fearsome head-cracking cudgel to be wielded against both human and animal attackers.

## Pray

Pray for those you know who are going through dark times at the moment. Ask God to give them the understanding that he is with them to rescue and protect.

*Lord, help me to trust in your goodness and guidance, even when you seem far away. Thank you for the way you have rescued and protected me, and help me to accept and grow under your loving discipline and care.*

# Feast before the foes

*For the sheep, there is always danger: extremes of cold and heat; the risks of constant travel and hungry predators. For the shepherd, this creates a dilemma.*

## An invitation

**Read Psalm 23:5**

❓ *We've already seen that God leads us to green pastures. What is different about this feast?*

The sheep must feed. To do this they must travel to find a good meadow or hill and be turned loose to graze. But among the green grass which beckons so invitingly grow poisonous plants that threaten health and well-being, even life. And predatory dangers lurk in the undergrowth all around. So the good shepherd prepares a table where the sheep may safely graze.

We too find ourselves surrounded by enemies of the soul. Some are strong, some are skilful, all are utterly ruthless. But Christ has overcome them all—their poison has been drawn, their power broken.

Even our great adversary has a fatal weakness. He has already been defeated! He is like a boxer who fights on because he will not admit he is beaten. Yet the judges have counted the scores and measured the match, and there is nothing he can do to alter the final verdict. He can still land a bruising blow—but he cannot overturn the result!

## ✓ Apply

Jesus has invited you to enjoy a banquet, even while enemies and dangers stand all around. It is part of the way he mocks those who imagine they can sneer and intimidate his people into silence or inactivity. As you drink from his word day by day; as you gather with his people; as you sing his praises; as you proclaim the goodness of the Good Shepherd in your walk and in your words, you are starting to taste the joyful feast that he has set before us.

## No more rations

**Re-read Psalm 23:5**

❓ *What is the significance of anointing a head with oil?*
❓ *What is symbolised by an overflowing cup?*

Honour, dignity, and chosen-ness are what anointing signifies. When we are in Christ, we share in his status as the chosen one— the Messiah. And God has given his Son all things. In Christ, we too have received all things. If you are a believer in Christ, you are, quite literally, a multi-billionaire; more wealthy than Gates or Bezos, Musk or Branson.

## ✓ Apply

❓ *Do you live knowing that you already have every spiritual blessing in Christ? What difference will that make today?*

# A sure future

*The man who wrote this psalm was no academic and lived no quiet, cloistered life. In his time he was a hero, traitor, giant-killer and an exile. He slept in fields, caves and palaces.*

## Confidence

### Read Psalm 23:6

❓ *What is David sure about and why?*

❓ *How do you think this confidence—faith—helped him deal with the highs and lows of his life?*

It isn't how much faith we have, but where we put it, that counts when everything turns against us. David's confidence did not grow out of his success or status. So when he lost those things, he found nothing essential had changed. His confidence was in something far more trustworthy and enduring: the character of God. So whatever the future held, he could look ahead and see that, for the rest of his life, he was in the care of a good and skilful shepherd. So long as he followed the Shepherd, goodness and mercy would follow him.

## ^ Pray

*Lord, teach me to know you better. Most of my greatest worries stem from the fact that I do not know who you really are. Since everything that matters depends on who you are—teach me to know you better. Then—whatever comes in this life—all will be well.*

## The party's over

❓ *What do you fear most about death?*

❓ *What do you imagine those around you think about death and the life beyond?*

Many things conspire to focus our attention on the short-term, on the here and now. This is not a bad thing—it is a good thing to be "in the moment" and engaged in the here and now. But unless we sometimes step back and look at the bigger picture, we may lose ourselves in the daily intricacies of life and miss the whole point of God's great scheme.

Some Bible critics say that the concept of eternity or the next life was a much later development in thinking, and that people in the Old Testament, like David, hoped to live on through their family and in the story of their lives, kept alive in the telling by the next generation. Many today share this view.

❓ *Would you say this is a reasonable interpretation of these verses?*

## ▽ Apply

As Billy Graham said: "I've read the last page of the Bible. It's all going to turn out all right." If you are a believer, you will live for ever in God's new creation.

❓ *How will this thought shape your own hopes and plans for the future?*

❓ *How will it shape what you do today?*

Talk to the Lord—the Good Shepherd—about your answers to these questions.

# RICH REFLECTION FOR EASTER

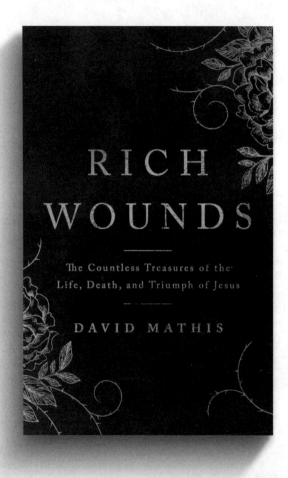

Many of us are so familiar with the Easter story that it becomes easy to miss subtle details as well as difficult to really enjoy its meaning. These 30 short but profound reflections will help you to pause and marvel at Jesus, whose now-glorified wounds are a sign of his unfailing love and the decisive victory that he has won. The readings will help you to meditate on the sacrificial love of Jesus at any time of year and especially but especially so at Easter.

**AVAILABLE NOW**

## thegoodbook.co.uk/rich-wounds
## thegoodbook.com/rich-wounds

# Introduce a friend to

## *explore*

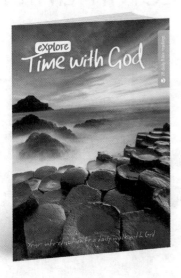

If you're enjoying using *Explore*, why not introduce a friend? *Time with God* is our introduction to daily Bible reading and is a great way to get started with a regular time with God. It includes 28 daily readings along with articles, advice and practical tips on how to apply what the passage teaches.

Why not order a copy for someone you would like to encourage?

# Coming up next...

- Nehemiah
  *with Eric Mason and Katy Morgan*

- Isaiah *with Tim Chester and Katy Morgan*

- Titus
  *with Nathan Buttery*

- Luke
  *with Tim Thornborough*

 Don't miss your copy. Contact your local Christian bookshop or church agent, or visit:

**UK & Europe:** thegoodbook.co.uk
info@thegoodbook.co.uk
Tel: 0333 123 0880

**North America:** thegoodbook.com
info@thegoodbook.com
Tel: 866 244 2165

**Australia & New Zealand:**
thegoodbook.com.au
info@thegoodbook.com.au
Tel: (02) 9564 3555

**India:** thegoodbook.co.in
info@thegoodbook.co.in
Tel: (+44) 0333 123 0880

**South Africa:** thegoodbook.co.za
info@thegoodbook.co.za

# Join the *explore* community

**The *Explore* Facebook group is a community of people who use *Explore* to study the Bible each day.**

This is the place to share your thoughts, questions, encouragements and prayers as you read *Explore*, and interact with other readers, as well as contributors, from around the world. No questions are too simple or too difficult to ask.

**JOIN NOW:**
facebook.com/groups/tgbc.explore